Practical worksheets, budgeting guides and up-to-date costs and industry information included inside!

5TH EDITION

RETAIL
in
DETAIL

RONALD L. BOND

Ep
Entrepreneur
PRESS®

Entrepreneur Press, Publisher
Cover Design: Beth Hansen-Winter
Production and Composition: Eliot House Productions

This publication is designed to provide accurate and authoritative information in
regard to the subject matter covered. It is sold with the understanding that the
publisher is not engaged in rendering legal, accounting, or other professional
services. If legal advice or other expert assistance is required, the services of a
competent professional person should be sought.

–From a Declaration of Principles jointly adopted by
a Committee of the American Bar Association and
a Committee of Publishers and Associations

Library of Congress Cataloging-in-Publication Data
Bond, Ronald L., 1939–
  Retail in detail / by Ronald L. Bond.—Fifth edition.
     p. cm.
  Includes index.
  ISBN 13: 978-1-59918-511-8 (alk. paper)
  ISBN 10: 1-59918-511-3 (alk. paper)
  1. Retail trade. 2. Small business. I. Title.
  HF5429.B6116 2013
  658.8'7—dc23

                                         2013011848

Printed in the United States of America

17 16 15 14 13   10 9 8 7 6 5 4 3 2 1

Contents

Contents	v

Part 1: Introduction

Since *Retail in Detail* was originally published in 1996, it has sold more than 25,000 copies in four editions, and established a reputation as a no-nonsense, down-to-earth guide for small retailers. It contains many specific examples and case studies, based on my experiences starting and successfully operating three retail stores and a bed-and-breakfast over a 20-year period.

This fifth edition retains the down-to-earth approach that has received positive reviews from both users and industry reviewers. It still includes worksheets that can be used by retailers to plan for and operate their businesses. It continues in the style of previous editions and makes liberal use of humor and personal experiences to illustrate important concepts.

In order to provide the latest up-to-date information, the entire book has been updated to reflect current conditions. References have been checked and modified to ensure that they are still current and valid.

In order to ensure that cost data is currently valid, dollar amounts included in the various worksheets and performance ratios were checked using Bureau of Labor Statistics cost indices for a number of items normally sold in small retail stores. The results show that, surprisingly, small retailing dollar values of the '90s are essentially the same, two decades later.

This verifies my own observations that items similar to the ones we sold in 1996 have not risen in price, but have actually declined in many cases. This is probably due to the increase in the number of items that are imported, and the general flattening of inflation in recent years due to monetary policy and the slow growth of the U.S. economy since the recession of 2008. While this is good news for consumers, it represents yet another challenge for small retailers struggling to maintain profit margins with flat prices and their own Increasing labor and utility expenses.

I hope this newly revised edition will prove valuable to you, whether you are considering opening a small retail store, or you are a new or experienced retailer who needs more information to help you operate your business.

Let the selling begin!

Chapter 1

What to Expect from This Book

I am assuming, since you have purchased or borrowed this book (or are surreptitiously reading it at your bookstore. . . Look out! The clerk is watching—better buy it now!), that you or someone you know is interested in becoming a retailer. I'm also assuming that you are planning on starting small and being actively involved in the business and that you would like to actually make a profit. Don't laugh: Some folks just want to keep busy, achieve tax deductions, or maintain a favorite hobby through owning a store. I'm also assuming that you are not planning to use this book to learn how to rise to the top of Walmart or JCPenney's. It's on a much more basic level than that.

If my assumptions are correct, once upon a time I was in your shoes. Writing a book about it, however, was the furthest thing from my mind when, in 1985, my wife, Susie, and I decided to open our own retail store. If you stick with me, I believe you will find the information I am about to share useful.

How We Learned the Hard Way

Before starting our store, we sought all available information and references that would help us navigate the maze of planning and startup. While we were able to obtain a lot of information, most of it was not directly applicable to small business retailing, nor was it specific enough to allow us to foresee and plan for the actual costs and events that materialized.

The Small Business Administration (SBA), for example, has a lot of information and many publications available for free. However, the government definition of "small business" covers companies with gross sales in the multiple millions of dollars. Many of the free pamphlets simply assume too large a scale of operation to be of any real use to a mom-and-pop retailer. Much of it also relates to manufacturing or service operations, which are also far removed from the reality of the small retail store we wanted to start.

We didn't want to use their retired business executive assistance program (called SCORE), because, frankly, we wanted to do it ourselves, our way, and really didn't want an outsider planning our shop. Ego aside, we also secretly feared that a rational, experienced businessperson might take one look at our plans and immediately fall into a fit of uncontrollable laughter at our ignorance and naiveté. This is not to minimize this resource; I'm sure these gentlemen and ladies are actually quite helpful and would never make fun of rookies such as us, but I guess we were a little apprehensive and perhaps too stubborn to admit we needed help.

In any event, we decided to proceed on our own, at our own pace, and desperately needed a how-to book, perhaps with a plain brown wrapper, that would give us detailed instructions on how to set up shop, without having to go public with our intentions. Alas! With the exception of one simplified accounting and finance handbook, we found no such resource.

We found plenty of books on business management in general, and others on how to get rich in real estate without investing a cent, but you can get this kind of information for free on early Sunday morning television infomercials. This kind of free information is usually worth exactly what you pay for it!

So, after finding out virtually everything by trial and error, I decided to try to fill this void in the information marketplace by writing down our experiences, our methods, and our failures so future entrepreneurs would have some footprints to follow, even though they may sometimes appear to have been left by a drunken sailor! Besides, with the eternal optimism of the entrepreneur I could see burgeoning book sales, huge royalties, autograph parties, talk show appearances. . . Whoa; back to earth! Where were we? Oh, yes, why I wrote this book!

So, if you are expecting a scholarly treatise on the science of retailing, instead of a commonsense, step-by-step instruction book on how to start a small retail store, you should probably look elsewhere.

Susie's and my objective was to combine her talents for decorating and crafts with my skills in business and management into a tangible enterprise that would also, hopefully, produce some extra income and provide a nest egg for retirement. Of course, we also harbored that secret dream of all entrepreneurs that our shop would prove wildly successful, be franchised nationwide, and make us millionaires by age 50. OK, so we got started a little late to fulfill our Horatio Alger fantasy by 30-something! Better late than never! In fact, retailing has become an attractive option for seniors who are at or near retirement and wish to keep busy, while earning supplemental retirement cash.

After more than 20 years in the retail business, we have yet to see our store name in lights in shopping centers across the nation, but we have successfully operated three retail stores and a bed-and-breakfast in two cities in the United States. We have achieved a degree of success that gave us some additional financial security in our "golden years." (We are now retired—well, almost.)

We have also gained a lot of experience, met many new and wonderful people (along with a few grouches), broadened our range of interests, and strengthened our relationship with each other and as a family. So we consider the venture a success. And even though we are not rich and famous yet, the first four editions of this book have sold more than 25,000 copies and we have received numerous testimonials from readers about how the book has helped them in their retail adventures. Neither of us had any real experience as retailers when we began, but we believed we had the basic ingredients for a successful store, if we planned carefully, were fiscally prudent, and executed our plans cautiously and deliberately.

Our family situation when we began was such that Susie could devote full time to the shop and I would be able to assist on a daily basis, while maintaining full-time outside employment. I also used vacation time to help during buying trips and at other times of peak need. The buying trips have proven to be what the Cajun people call "lagniappe"—something special and extra that is not expected. We have had many wonderful trips together all over the United States. We had two sons, one working part time and attending the local community college and the other in high school when we started. Both have completed their educations and have now started families and careers of their own.

We began serious planning for our first store in spring 1985, opened it in September, and operated it successfully for 14 years through a period of changing economic climate. In spring 1991, we began planning for our second store, which we opened in August 1991, in a shopping center across town from the first. In 1998, we closed this second store. In 1999, we moved to our eventual retirement location and opened another store, combined with a bed-and-breakfast. In 2000, we sold our first store and, in 2001, we closed the last store and B&B. Since then, we have maintained a foothold in the retailing arena by operating several booths in cooperative markets, as well as speaking to and advising other retailers.

Through these experiences, which can best be characterized as trial and error, we developed a reliable operating philosophy, established a credible reputation in the community, and achieved a degree of financial success, which we are attempting to share in this volume. It is our hope that the book will help you as you chart your own course into the business of retailing.

How Information Is Organized in This Book

Since I was educated as an engineer, my thinking is pretty linear. Susie has other words to describe it, sometimes, but let's not get into name calling! Accordingly, the material is presented generally in the order in which you are likely to need it, starting with a brief overview of small retailing and proceeding through research and planning, opening and managing your store(s), and finally, closing or selling your business. I've also included appendices containing useful reference materials.

Interspersed throughout the book are worksheets, tables, and figures designed to provide actual tools you can use to plan and manage your retail business. Feel free to photocopy and use them as needed.

Having made the point about sequential organization, let me also note that retailing, as life in general, does not lend itself to neat chronological sequences. Some subjects pop up unexpectedly and some issues recur throughout the business cycle. So some subjects are organized into what I considered the most appropriate chapter, rather than in strict logical sequence. All this is to say that you should read the entire book before proceeding with your plans.

Throughout the book, I have attempted to share our specific experiences relating to our retailing operations. They are identified in sidebars captioned "Our Experience."

Other than this device, I have tried to avoid the "CNN method" of presenting information. There are no bottom-line crawls of unrelated data on each page. I have not used tired graphics or *"factoids"* encased in text boxes containing tips and trivia that are, well, trivial, just to provide eye candy. I am assuming that your attention span is greater than a turnip's and that you are capable of following a logical sequence of thought for more than a few seconds. If I am wrong, I am also writing a comic book. . .

Oh, yes, if you find a term that is unfamiliar, look it up in the Glossary included as Appendix A.

History and Current State of Retailing

B efore we get down to the nitty-gritty of starting your store, it is appropriate to step back a little and get an overview of retailing. How did retailing develop? What is it now?

History of Retailing

Remember I told you this would not be a scholarly, academic book? Well, here is my personal version of the history of retailing.

In prehistoric times, when Grog the caveman (the consumer) became hungry, he grabbed his club and headed out to find the nearest wooly mammoth (the manufacturer), whacked it over the head, carved out as many wooly mammoth steaks as he could carry, and brought them home to Mrs. Grog to cook and serve to the family. The food lasted for several days (unless there were cave-teens in the family, in which case it was gone in several seconds).

This system worked pretty well. Mrs. Grog liked the fact that Grog was kept busy getting food, preventing him from hanging out with the single cavemen at the local campfire down the canyon. However, there were negatives. The menu selection was limited. Mrs. Grog was also kept busy preparing large quantities of the same food, often developing headaches, thereby endangering the future of the human race. When the food ran out and Grog returned to the wooly mammoth carcass, he often found, sadly, that the "use by" date had passed or that a group of semi-human scavengers (called "telemarketers") had devoured the remaining scraps.

Grog's brother-in-law, Sars, often dropped in at supper time and observed the situation. He saw the inefficiencies in the system and soon devised a process in which he would become an "intermediary" by hiring his cousin Rawbuck to kill wooly mammoths and drag the carcasses to a nearby glacier. There, Sars would divide them into steaks, chops, roasts, ground meat, and franks, ice them down, and sell them in small manageable quantities to Grog and the other cave-consumers, maintaining a small profit margin for himself. Sars and Rawbuck soon formed a partnership and hung up a sign—and the first retail store was born. They later expanded their offerings to hardware, power tools, appliances, and soft goods and opened multiple outlets across the United Cave States. And that's the history of retailing in a nutshell!

On a more scholarly note, according to the website, retail industry.about.com, the word "retail" is derived from the French word *retaillier,* meaning to cut a piece off or to break bulk. So, my working definition of retailing would be the process or system by which large quantities of goods or services are broken down and repackaged, perhaps several times, into a quantity or form that is readily usable by the end consumer. The system usually involves the manufacturer or source, along with intermediate wholesalers or jobbers, and finally, the local retail store that you are considering opening.

Current State of Retailing

Today, retailing has evolved into a complex system of supply and demand impacted by quickly changing technology and trends. At its core, however, it is still the buying of wooly mammoths, carving them up into consumer-sized chunks, and selling them at a small profit. Note that I said small profit. More about that later.

One recent trend that has affected retailing tries to bring the manufacturer or wholesaler directly to the consumer via "big-box" stores, such as Walmart, Costco, and Sam's Club. Also part of this trend is internet selling, or e-tailing, along with the increase of TV and catalog sales. Although the specific methodologies and technologies differ, the goal of this movement is to eliminate retailers and thus secure a greater share of profits for the manufacturers and wholesalers. For some products, and some consumers, it is working, and some retailers are being hurt by this growing trend.

A counter trend, however, is working against the wholesaling approach. Today's consumer increasingly demands top-quality merchandise, a large selection, individual service, and convenience. Providing this through the wholesaling or impersonal-technology approach is not easy, although many of the mass marketers are becoming more innovative in meeting these needs.

One limitation on the wholesaling approach is shipment and delivery. Even though items can be viewed and ordered on the internet, they must still be shipped to you; this involves delay and expense. It is still cheaper to ship in bulk than in individual packages, so costs increase when items are shipped to individual addresses, rather than to a store. It also involves potential problems with sizing, differences between photos and actual appearance, and the inherent human need to touch and feel merchandise before purchasing.

A social issue spawned by the wholesaling trend is impulse and overbuying. We all know someone who has a closet full of stuff bought on impulse on QVC, Home Shopping Network, or eBay.

> **Our Experience**
>
> Susie took away my Sam's Club card and forbade me to go there after I bought 50 pounds of par-boiled rice and several huge boxes of cereal that would not fit in our pantry! Sometimes large-quantity buying does not make sense.

One need only look at recent retailing success stories such as Starbucks and Barnes & Noble to see that specialty retailers that provide quality products, available in customer-desired varieties, styles, and flavors and sold in customer-friendly venues, are still achieving spectacular successes.

To summarize the current state of retailing, I would say that technology and other trends are changing its face, but innovative, specialty retailers that are focused on current customer desires instead of relying on past experience will still succeed in today's marketplace.

Chapter 3

The Future
of Retailing in the
Electronic Age

What's in Store (Pun Intended)
for the Future?

The short answer is "I don't really know." But I think we can draw some conclusions based on past and current trends.

♦ Technology and transportation advances will continue to change the ways in which we get our goods and services.
♦ Internet, TV, and catalog sales will probably increase for some consumers and some products.
♦ Renting a space and setting the same old stuff on the shelves will not work anymore.
♦ It will be necessary to become more agile in responding to customer desires. Tomorrow's retailers must position themselves to respond quickly to the changing market environment. This means keeping up with your industry trends and doing your own research.

- There is still a niche for "the better mousetrap" in products, services, and style. Innovation will be mandatory.
- More affluent consumers will demand better, more specialized, more individualized, and more convenient ways of shopping.
- Successful retailers must get to know their customers and anticipate their needs.
- Retailers may need to adopt more than one selling method to succeed, e.g., sell on the internet or by catalog as well as maintain a static location.

On balance, I believe retailing is here to stay. In some ways, the more things change, the more they stay the same. Even in today's high-tech world, most consumers still go to supermarkets, department stores, clothing stores, and many specialty retail stores. Even with the growing availability of internet chat rooms, dating services, and mail-order brides, most people still want to meet their mates the old-fashioned way, so they can experience firsthand the sights, sounds, and emotions of selecting a life partner. I believe we will want to do the same with our goods-and-services selections.

Meeting Consumer Needs vs. Selling a Product

Humans are social beings, with an innate need for contact with other humans. Ironically, the technology (internet, TV and telephone shopping, texting, telecommuting) that tends to isolate us from actual physical contact may actually promote the local retail store as a place where consumers can fulfill their need for human contact while also meeting their needs for personal and household products. It will be up to enterprising retailers to fashion their venues in ways that meet these changing needs.

Barnes and Nobles, Starbucks, internet cafes, sports bars, and grills are examples of how retail stores have successfully catered to this need. These venues not only offer products for sale, they offer comfortable, relaxing, environments for consumers to interact, have fun, and relate to other people while shopping. These stores offer such amenities as wifi, large screen TVs, children's play areas, information kiosks, and accessory products for sale.

The successful retailer of the future will be one who observes the changes occurring in our society, and crafts a store environment that accommodates those changes. Ideally, that environment will provide interaction, recreation, and a comfortable, relaxing venue for shopping, as well as quality merchandise. You do not need to reinvent the wheel or be a futurist. Simply observe successful retailers and emulate their methods. The large chains spend millions on focus groups and market research, before establishing their retailing models. You can benefit from their efforts by simply becoming a careful observer of what is working and what is not in your local mall or strip center.

Part 2: Decisions Must Be Made!

Chapter 4

Is Retailing Really for You?

Assessing the Realities

It's scary to invest your savings in a new venture that, according to statistics, has less than a 50 percent chance to survive two years or more. That fancy word, "entrepreneur," really means a risk taker, one who is willing to gamble that he or she can beat the odds and provide services or goods that will meet the needs or wants of that fickle entity, the consumer, and that the consumer will shell out enough hard-earned dollars to keep the enterprise solvent. Starting your own business is not quite like putting your quarter in a slot machine but there are some similarities! You do have a better chance of controlling the odds if you plan carefully, but the jackpot of success does depend, to some extent, on forces beyond your direct control.

In view of these sobering realities, you will do well to spend plenty of time talking through your idea and doing some soul searching. Remember the song from *The Music Man*, when Professor Harold Hill asks the parents to observe their sons for "the telltale signs of corruption:" "Are certain words creeping into his conversation, words like 'Swell!' and 'So's your old man'?" Well, check your own conversation and see if phrases such as the following are creeping in. If so, beware! The entrepreneurial bug may have bitten you!

- Why shouldn't I devote my time and talents to building my own business?
- I'm tired of the stress of the rat race.
- I want to be my own boss!
- I want to invest my time and money in an enterprise that will help get the kids through college.
- I want a change in lifestyle.
- I want to get rich quick.

You've probably heard or said all of the above or you wouldn't be reading this book. All of them, and many more, are perfectly good reasons for starting a business—*except the last one!* Based on our limited experience, not only will you not get rich quickly, you probably never will, unless you just happen to have the recipe for a great-tasting ice cream that is determined by the surgeon general to be a sure-fire cure for obesity. In all likelihood, however, you can gradually increase your earnings to help out with the household expenses and, if you're persistent and perhaps a little lucky, you can build your business to fully support your family. Don't give up the big dream, but don't expect it to happen overnight!

As you ponder whether or not to take the plunge, here are some questions you have to answer for yourself:

- Do I really want to do this?
- Does my family situation allow me to spend a *large* amount of time on a business?
- Do I have the right personality for retailing?
- Do I have or can I get the financial resources?
- What happens if the business fails?

The point at which you stop talking and start doing varies, but seems to occur with some regularity during the much-celebrated midlife crisis period.

This is a time when many people pause to take stock of their lives. After taking inventory, many people decide they haven't accomplished all they intended to do by that stage of life. You may have decided that you are tired of the rat race and want to chuck it all for life as a beachcomber, get an extreme makeover, buy a new sports car, or one of the other equally insane things people do. After looking at your teenage kids, who are to your money as a vacuum cleaner is to lint, you settle for "starting your own business." Probably a wise decision, considering the alternatives.

You may also be stuck in a job or profession that seems to be a dead end or that is not providing you the satisfaction or financial rewards you expect from life. Or, you may be one of the increasing number of middle and upper managers who have been laid off or retired early, as part of the seemingly endless downsizing of corporate America.

At some point, you have to stop talking and start doing. You can't keep dipping your toes in the water and pulling back; you've got to jump in sometime or get off the beach!

The next section will help you evaluate the good and bad aspects of retailing as we have experienced them and perhaps help you make that decision.

Psychological Demands of Retail

There are a lot of publications available that attempt to help you determine if

> **Our Experience**
>
> Prior to starting our first store, we talked for years about starting various enterprises, even did some investigations and made some tentative moves, but always pulled back short of actually committing to a business—sort of like sticking your toe in the water at the beach and drawing back to safety and comfort because the water is dark and cold. As a result, we saw others actually start businesses we had talked about—and succeed.

your personality is well suited to being in business, but since I'm not a psychologist, I won't attempt to test your personal aptitude for business. There are published question lists that purport to determine your suitability specifically for retailing. The free Small Business Administration materials on this subject are probably as good as any. If you're like me, you probably won't be deterred by a negative score anyway, if you really want to own a business.

This is not to say that you should not consider very carefully whether or not your temperament is suited to operating a retail business. I will attempt to give you a truthful portrait of our experiences, both good and bad, from which you can assess your own aptitude for enduring the retailing life. I just won't try to "psych you out" by making you answer a lot of questions such as "Did you hate your mother?"

If you are a generally well-adjusted person (whatever that means) who enjoys dealing with people, has average intelligence, and is not crushed by failure, you probably have the basic psychological equipment. But I hereby disclaim any responsibility for your decision! On some days, I don't even accept responsibility for my own decision, preferring instead to plead insanity!

The Good, the Bad, and the Ugly

Here are some of the things we liked best and least about operating retail stores.

The good:

- Working together as a team (most of the time!)
- The feeling of "ownership" of a community enterprise
- Meeting people and making new friends
- Going on buying trips (and charging them off as a legitimate business expense)
- A feeling of control over at least a part of your life
- Compliments on how nice the shop looks
- Christmas sales figures
- Taking a few bucks out of the business now and then
- Learning that most people are basically honest and trustworthy

The bad:

- Keeping up with all the bureaucratic paperwork
- Children who pick up and destroy things while parents blithely ignore them

◆ Customers who complain about price or think they can "make this" and blatantly make notes on how to copy your merchandise
◆ January sales figures
◆ The endless buy-sell-buy-sell cycle
◆ Realizing that your large bank balance is mostly accounts payable
◆ Taking inventory
◆ Taking down the Christmas decorations
◆ Putting up the Christmas decorations
◆ Cleaning the restroom, vacuuming, and dusting (just like at home)
◆ Discovering an empty clothes hanger hidden behind a cabinet and realizing that you've been visited by a shoplifter
◆ Getting that large check back marked "Insufficient Funds" or "Account Closed"

The ugly:

◆ Realizing that you never get to enjoy holidays as you used to, because you are working
◆ Coming to work and finding the plate glass window smashed and items missing from your store
◆ Firing or laying off an employee
◆ Staring at that large display of items you were sure would fly out the door—but are all still there two months later

So, there they are! Only you can decide if these pluses and minuses, taken together, will fit into your vision of your preferred lifestyle. One final word of caution: if you don't enjoy people, including meeting and dealing with them on a daily basis, then retailing is probably not the business for you.

Get Informed

IBM's famous slogan, "Plan Ahead," was never more applicable than in starting a retail shop. Time, effort, and a few dollars invested in planning will pay large dividends later on. Earlier we discussed the need to make a commitment at some point. While it's one thing to jump into the water, it's another thing to jump naked into freezing water without knowing how to swim. In other words, while there is always some risk, you should spend the time needed to become informed on the business you're about to enter, learn how it operates, and thus increase your survival chances.

After making a decision to open a store, you should set target action dates that will allow plenty of time for research and preparation, but not so far in the future that you fail to take the commitment seriously.

I will recount some of the things we did that were helpful and that we recommend as preludes to the actual opening. Obviously, there are several decision points at which you can abort the process without serious financial loss. Prudence dictates that you consider these go/no-go decisions carefully, in light of information you have obtained. However, I strongly urge you not to enter into this phase of the process with the idea in mind that you can always call it quits if something discouraging turns up—something always does! It is very important to make a definite commitment at this stage and call it off only in the face of serious and multiple problems. You will never succeed at anything if you don't make a decision and stick to it. I can assure you that there will be land mines and other unpleasant and unanticipated obstacles that you will encounter, and only the truly committed will have the resolve to carry on.

> **Our Experience** ● When we opened our first store, we set a goal of opening about five months in the future and scheduled our activities to meet that date.

Enough of this lecture on commitment! The Bible sums it up well: "No one who puts his hand to the plow and looks back is fit for service. . ." LUKE 9:62 (KJV).

You're probably tired of being preached at by now, so let's get to the activities that I would suggest for the planning period.

Research Available Resources

Begin by visiting your local bookstores and libraries to find books and magazines that deal with your proposed area of business.

(You've obviously already taken this advice or you wouldn't be reading this.) A list of books and magazines on retailing and small businesses is included in Appendix B. If you can't find them locally, subscribe or write for sample copies. Some of them may be available online. Mentioned earlier, there are not a lot of references that will give you the detailed, specific data you will need (other than this book, of course!), but it is helpful to study the magazines and books related to small businesses in general and the material on related business operations.

Don't ignore the internet as a source for information, but take it with a grain of salt. Remember all those emails about lost little girls, government activities that threaten our freedoms, and celebrity statements that turned out to be urban legends or downright lies? Be sure to check out internet sources before swallowing the information provided. Having said that, "googling" your retailing area of interest will probably turn up several legitimate sources of information, including, hopefully, the title of this book. Internet research can be the fastest way to narrow down information resources.

If you are planning on starting your business in a locale other than where you live and with which you are familiar, you can obtain valuable information from travel and regional magazines and books. You should also write to or find the website for the Chamber of Commerce in the target city and use it to download or ask for information on the business activity, major industries, schools, and anything else you believe will give you some insight into the business climate in which you will be operating. Consider subscribing to the local newspaper. It can give you lots of information on space availability, costs, state of the local economy, etc. In short, a few dollars and a little effort expended here can yield large dividends of information.

Don't expect the information to be indexed and catalogued to your specific needs. You will have to spend many hours digging it out and interpreting it as it relates to your business plans. Real estate agents and such will sometimes offer to do your research for you. This is OK, but don't get lazy and totally rely on such information, because, even if it is technically correct, it is designed to sell property or rent space, not ensure that your business is successful. That's your job—and you can't get out of it!

The Small Business Administration (SBA) has lots of resources for small retailers. By visiting their website at www.sba.gov, you will have access to resources covering various areas of retailing, training courses, and checklists designed to assess your own abilities. SBA also offers periodic seminars at locations across the United States. Appendix B has a list of some of the available resources.

Our Experience We found the SBA seminar on starting your own business that we attended to be helpful, in a general sense, but it failed to give us the specific information we wanted.

Call your local IRS office and arrange to attend one of the free seminars that they offer on small business tax matters. We attended an IRS seminar and received some valuable information on the kinds of taxes you will have to pay, but we were not particularly impressed with the quality of the presentation.

Our Experience If you are going into business as a husband/wife team or with a partner, it is helpful to divide up these preliminary duties according to your individual interests and skills. That way, you can cover more ground in less time.

Divide research up with your partner along areas of interest. I have aptitudes and training in management and finance, while Susie is the creative and imaginative partner, so we divided up the responsibilities along those lines.

Check Out the Competition

One of the best ways to become informed is to visit shops similar to the kind you want to open. Look, write down your impressions, and ask questions of the shop owner, if possible. A word of caution here! Don't go into shops in the same area in which you plan to locate and expect merchants to spill their guts to you on how to compete with them! Ask questions only in areas far enough away that you will not be in competition.

Interviewing existing shop owners may be the most fertile ground for good information, although it does take more effort to seek out and obtain. Write down your questions before you talk to the shop owners and take time to jot down the answers as soon as possible after or even during the conversation. Otherwise, you may lose valuable information in the excitement of the moment.

You should also survey your area to get an idea of space availability and costs. You can do this by checking your newspaper or calling a commercial leasing agent. We'll discuss this in more detail in a later chapter, but now is the time to get acquainted with general space availability and cost.

> **Our Experience**
>
> When we visited shops similar to ours, we found that it was best to approach the owners directly, be honest about our intentions, and ask for their advice. We assured them we did not intend to compete in their sales area. We found that most retail shop owners will help with a lot of useful information, if they are approached in a non-threatening way. After all, who doesn't like to talk about their business? Some folks even write books about it!

Let's assume that you have decided that retailing suits your needs and lifestyle and you've done your research in checking out the territory in your chosen area of operation. Now it's time to get down to specifics and get that store open!

Chapter 5

Planning for Your Business

I f ever there was a business in which it is easy to fall into the trap of "not seeing the forest for the trees," it is retailing. It is a business in which you live or die with each day's sales. This is doubly true if you own and manage a retail store. Why is this so?

An article ridiculing the fancy job descriptions that bureaucrats create for themselves gave the following description: "The incumbent in this position makes irrevocable decisions involving interstate commerce. Decisions must be made immediately and are not subject to review by higher authority. Wrong decisions can result in millions of dollars in damages." What was this seemingly high-level executive job? The description was for a flagger on a highway construction project.

While this job description obviously exaggerates the importance of the flagger, it can certainly be applied to a retail store owner. That is why it is so hard to keep a global perspective when you are in the midst of an operation in which you must make instant decisions, take sole responsibility for them, and see the results at the end of each and every day in the form of the day's sales. Is it any wonder that you feel like you are on an emotional roller coaster? During your first few months in business, you will likely go home either depressed or elated because of the day's receipts.

Perhaps no other business has as many variables and so much unpredictability that gets translated into such immediate, measurable results. In manufacturing, you have contracts on which you can plan for months or even years. In a service business, you book your work in advance. But in retailing, you open the store each day, without any earthly idea who will come, whether they will buy anything, and if you will cover expenses. While there are seasonal sales cycles, you have absolutely no way of knowing what a particular day or week will bring in the way of sales. You are literally at the mercy of the weather, changing trends, and the idiosyncrasies of individual people.

Are they in a buying mood or not? Will today's good weather motivate them to shop or to go to the lake? Is this payday for a lot of people? Is the national economy in a recession or a boom? What did the stock market do today? The answers to these and a hundred other questions hold the key to your sales volume for a given day and can determine your mood unless you take a longer perspective.

Our Experience ● One phenomenon we observed over the years is that sales at our stores generally ran counter to national retailing statistics, i.e., when retail sales are down on the national level, ours were frequently up, and vice versa. While I am certainly no economist, I have postulated that since the national retail sales figures include many large-ticket items, such as appliances and even automobiles, consumers who decide they cannot afford the big purchases may increase their spending on lower-cost personal or decorative items to compensate. Conversely, when their focus is on larger items, they tend to buy fewer everyday things in order to save for the big-ticket purchases. I do not have any hard numbers to back up "Bond's Theory of Inverse Sales," so don't build your business plan around it!

Develop a Business Plan

After this seemingly bleak picture of the unpredictability of retailing, you may wonder if there is any valid reason for attempting to do any business planning. The answer is a resounding "Yes!" Even though there is little predictability from day to day or even week to week, you can count on patterns in overall consumer demand and the buying habits of consumers in general. This means that, unless you are in a totally atypical selling environment, you will be able to count on and plan for a reasonably stable demand for your products, provided you have done a good job of selecting a product line and location.

The key is not to become mired in the emotions of daily sales figures, but to plan for the long term and carry through with those plans despite the daily seesawing of receipts.

An old proverb states that if you don't have any particular destination, you should have no trouble getting there. You should, therefore, develop a business plan, set some goals and objectives, and craft a reporting system to tell you if your plan is succeeding. This business plan includes the planning, researching, and forecasting discussed in earlier chapters. But your plan should also set some goals with respect to the overall results you expect to achieve. You should be able to answer these questions:

◆ What level of sales do you expect to reach in the first year?
◆ What percent of growth do you want for each succeeding year?
◆ How much profit do you want to make the first year and thereafter?

You may say you have no idea how to predict such things, but you must if you are to intelligently plan your business operation. Do some research at your library, talk with other merchants, consult national business periodicals, and set some realistic but challenging goals. Don't think too small, since most people seldom rise above their expectations.

Monitor Your Progress

Once you set your goals, implement a system to monitor your progress. Keep up with sales on a monthly and quarterly basis, along with expenses and profit margins. Compare the results with your plan. If you meet your goals, celebrate—go out for dinner. If

Our Experience

When we started our business, we set a goal of increasing our sales 10 percent a year and maintaining net profit margins between 10 percent and 15 percent. We generally achieved our sales goals, but we remained on the low end of the profit range. As we perceived that we were falling short of our goals, we took steps to improve. We moved our location after three years to get in a higher-traffic location and save on rent. We worked on improving our gross profit by trying to include freight costs in our markup, where possible. We also increased our emphasis on advertising to try to keep up with our plan to increase sales.

you don't meet them, don't panic. Remember that you should not place too much stock in short-term performance, because it can be skewed by so many of the factors mentioned above. If, on the other hand, you are actually falling behind, try to make adjustments to your operation.

If sales are lower than planned, explore the possibility of increasing your advertising. If your profit margin is lower than planned, take a look at your pricing policies to see if you can improve profit without affecting sales by raising prices just slightly. Look into the possibility of moving your store or opening other outlets. After all your investigations, you may discover a reason beyond your control, such as worsening local economic conditions.

Check with other merchants to see if they are having the same experience. If so, maybe the only thing to do is hunker down, cut expenses as much as you can, and ride it out. Remember: in selling as in physics, what goes up must come down, and vice versa. You can at least be positioned to take advantage of the upturn when it does occur.

The point is, you should have projections and plans for your business. If you achieve them, great! If not, you will be in a better position to make corrections or to roll with the punches you can't control or anticipate. Step back from the trees and take a look at the forest. Remember: You are not in business for a day or a week, but for the long haul. You need to keep that all-important perspective.

Keep Up with Changing Trends

Have you ever walked into a store and felt that you had entered a reverse time warp into yesterday? Unfortunately, some retailers who have had some success in the past believe that they can continue to be successful by doing the same things. You've heard the old saying that you can't get anywhere by whipping a dead horse? Well, some folks believe that there's no horse too dead to beat.

In today's market, customers demand an up-to-date shopping environment as well as a good product line. Don't be lulled into a false sense of security by assuming that things will stay as they are now. Try to anticipate changes in demand for your products and then modify or update your product line accordingly. Equally as important, change and update your displays and store ambiance to accommodate changing customer needs. This costs money, but it is an investment in your future viability. You should consider a major remodeling at least every five years and do other minor redecorating, such as new paint or wallpaper, more frequently.

The reason that Barnes & Noble bookstores have achieved such success is not that they necessarily have more and better books than the old corner bookstore. A lot of their appeal has to do with their store layout, their amenities for lounging and reading books, and their coffee bars and cafes. Would you rather shop for books in a pleasant, airy, inviting area, while sipping a cappuccino, or wander along cramped, musty bookshelves, sneezing?

Try to see your store as your customers see it and ask what you can do to make it more inviting. Don't be afraid to try something new, even if it is a lot different from what you have been doing. The seven last words of any organization are "We never did it that way before."

Continuing Education

Hopefully, this book will fill in many of the gaps in your information as a novice entrepreneur and provide guidance as you contemplate whether or not retailing is for you. As you plan and make your entry into the most treasured American dream, owning your own business, you will still face many unanswered questions and problems. However, you will also receive many rewards.

Starting and managing a Sears store is a great deal different from struggling, with limited resources, to open a small mom-and-pop retail store. While the principles are the same, it is somewhat intimidating to try to follow Harvard Business School instructions when you know in your heart that you are not, and probably never will be, a business mogul.

In your venture, you will need to deal with more clear, down-to-earth solutions and specific details of starting a small business, complete with the frustrations, difficulties, and rewards "thereunto appertaining," as they say on those MBA diplomas. All of the answers are not in this book, but if you continue the learning process on your own and are always willing and eager to listen to new and different ideas, you will have what it takes to survive.

Nurturing your business will require considerable time and effort—and you will ask yourself many times if it is worth it. You will talk about selling out, usually right after a particularly trying day at work or in a cash-flow crunch.

Our Experience ● After more than 16 years, we eventually reached the point where we felt we were ready to quit. Reaching our desired retirement age and starting to have grandchildren had a lot to do with that decision. However, neither of us regrets the years we spent in retailing. The reasons we enjoyed the experience are complex and not easily put into words. We were successful in the sense that we always showed a profit, but the amount of the profits has not always been as great as we wanted. We liked the work, generally, but it also got tiring and sometimes very b-o-r-i-n-g. We were able to use proceeds from our business to help put our children through college and help them with their finances early in their marriages. No, we're not rich, but despite some of the downsides, we have been able to retire somewhat earlier than we would have otherwise.

The main reason entrepreneurs stick with it has to do with a sense of accomplishment and pride of ownership you will get from no other venture. You will be proud of your business that you actually started from scratch—a business that you are maintaining and people really seem to like and are willing to support with their money. You will also like attaining a certain measure of control over your life, unlike what you would get from a conventional job that puts you in a position of subservience to an organization whose goals and objectives may or may not coincide with your own.

As people approach that midlife point, begin to evaluate their accomplishments to date, and compare their ultimate goals with the time remaining to achieve them, they generally conclude that there is a gap between expectations and reality. Owning your own business provides an alternative means of accomplishment.

In addition, you will enjoy the opportunity to become a part of a community, by meeting and establishing friendships with many people with whom you would otherwise not have come in contact. Other, more direct benefits are opportunities to work closely with others, such as your spouse, traveling to the merchandise markets, and getting to see more of this country.

Although you probably will not become rich, you may be able to use your profits to help with family finances, supplement college expenses, and most importantly, build an equity that will hopefully be available to provide for some extra security in your retirement years.

Lest you fixate on this euphoric ending and ride off into the sunset, a more honest appraisal is that, for all you will gain from this experience, you will also have to give up some things—things like freedom to take vacations when other "normal" people do, being home for supper with the family every night, and being available for your kids as much as you would like. If you have older children, you can probably maintain a reasonably good relationship with them, but if you have young children, retailing may result in your spending less time with them than they need in order to cope successfully with the trials of childhood or adolescence.

Seven Planning Do's and Don'ts

1. Do evaluate your reasons for wanting to start a business.
2. Do be realistic about the cost of starting a business and be sure you are capable of acquiring the necessary funds.
3. Do evaluate the personal cost of investing a good portion of your life in a business.
4. Do try to apply the information contained in this book to your own personal situation, instead of assuming that what worked for one business will work for you.
5. Don't be intimidated by the statistics about business failures, if you really want to try.
6. Don't listen to all the free advice you will get from those who have never gotten into the game or have dropped out.
7. Don't give up too easily, after you start.

Now, it is up to you!

Chapter 6

What Will
You Sell?

The Selection Process

The fact that you are reading this book means that you are probably interested in selling something to someone. The "something" is known as your product and the "someone" is your target market. You may have a really firm idea about what you intend to sell or you may be casting about for just the right product, or line of products, that will fulfill your needs.

As you look around at the seemingly limitless array of products that are available for sale in even the smallest town or city, you may be overwhelmed by the task of choosing your product. Or, you may find, as we did when we first started thinking about going into business, that you are constantly identifying and discarding products or product lines. Don't dismay! This is a necessary part of your search for a product line that meets the needs of your proposed customers, as well as suiting your own abilities to secure and market it.

Remember that your first choice is not cast in stone. Although your choice of a product line does influence your decisions about location, means of selling, and design of your facility, you are free to make changes to your line after you open and gauge the reaction of your market. Such changes should normally be well reasoned and

Our Experience ● We went through a large number of products, from frozen yogurt to fabrics, before we finally settled on our final choice of country gifts and accessories.

evolutionary, not revolutionary, or else you will confuse your customers and be seen as someone who is constantly changing to suit each minor shift in the winds of commerce.

In order for your store to be successful, your product line must meet two critical tests. One, it must be merchandise for which a demand exists or can be created. Two, it must suit your own talents and abilities to obtain and market. In addition to these two basic criteria, you must also consider the competitive environment and the profitability of the products.

Consumer Demand

First, let's examine the question of demand. As mentioned above, demand can exist already or it can be created. Catering to an existing demand requires less effort at marketing, but usually involves more competition for consumer dollars. On the other hand, creating a new market is more difficult and requires more advertising and education of consumers, but it offers the advantage of a "captive market," until the point when other retailers realize you are successful and start to compete with you. Notice, I said "when" not "if." Competition is inevitable when you are successful.

Take, for example, the movie rental market. It's obvious that a demand exists. In the 1980s, video rental stores popped up in every neighborhood. By the middle of the 1990s, they had almost all disappeared, replaced by large stores such as Blockbuster, which offered better service and larger selections. By 2010, most of these big stores had also followed the dinosaurs into extinction (Blockbuster went into bankruptcy and was bought by DISH Network in 2012). Their replacement was by-mail video rental companies such as Netflix. Mail-order movie rentals have now fallen victim to online streaming videos and on-demand movies on consumers' TVs, tablets, laptops, and smartphones.

So, even if a large demand exists, success is not guaranteed for the small retailer. Products with high demand often attract too much interest and technology from the well-capitalized large companies to allow a small operator to compete successfully.

This particular market also illustrates another inevitability: Change will always come and you will not always be able to anticipate it. The best you can do is be ready to adapt when the new marketing environment emerges. When marketing a product that has broad appeal to consumers, it pays to remain as flexible as possible and be able to adapt with minimal expense. Chapter 24 gives some tips for anticipating and managing change.

Markets can also be created. This is done most often by importing a product or product line to your area from another area where it has already proven to be a good seller. Be careful, here, though, because a regional product may not be readily transplantable. Grits cookers may not find ready acceptance north of the Mason-Dixon Line and Pennsylvania scrapple would likely be a hard sell in the South. Even if you were to be successful in

We found this out the hard way, when we attempted to introduce to the Southwest new lines of country products that were popular on the East Coast. We found the consumers just weren't educated in the new looks enough to make them profitable.

transferring a "foreign" product, it may take too long to build the market in your area to have a viable business.

Some styles and looks are just not transferable. For instance, we have found that certain California products seem to appeal only to Californians, perhaps because of unique lifestyles and environment. Most of these non-transplantable products seem to fall in the categories of decorating, furniture, and ethnic foods.

Some products seem to be readily transferable, such as kids' toys, novelty and health foods, and entertainment products. If, on your visits to other parts of the country, you see a product that is popular in a couple of diverse cultures, it probably will sell in your area and you should consider it a likely candidate. Generally with

Our Experience ● This happened to us with frozen yogurt. We were living in Tennessee, and on a visit to Arkansas, discovered the frozen dessert when it was first being introduced. We agonized so long in making our decision that someone else opened a store nearby, while we were still making our minds up. It was very successful for a long time. With the advent of light ice cream, and a trend toward food that tastes good, regardless of its healthiness or fat content, the appeal of frozen yogurt waned somewhat. With the recent obesity epidemic resulting from our "super-size –it" mentality, and with a new self-serve store format featuring a large number of flavors and toppings, it seems to be making a comeback, illustrating that nothing lasts forever, and that demand tends to run in cycles. In any event, when it comes to hot new products, he who hesitates is lost.

such products, you should move promptly to introduce them or someone will beat you to the punch.

There's a third category of products—those that are introduced in one locality and then move across the country in waves, following general fashion trends. This has been a noticeable phenomenon in the country decorating arena. Most country and craft trends, we found, seem to begin in the Carolinas, Tennessee, and California and then expand slowly.

Sometimes, it's a matter of introducing a product before its time has come. If you have the patience and market it aggressively, using magazines and other means to show its acceptance in other areas, you may be successful in hurrying the process. With other items, it may be best to wait until the trend catches up with your location.

For a new store, you would be wise to stick to known sellers for most of your stock and worry about becoming a trendsetter only after you are well established. In any event, you should keep up with trends in other parts of the country so you can introduce new products when the time is ripe.

The best of both these worlds occurs when you can identify a product line that is selling well in your town, but that is available only in a small part of the retail trade area. Then you have the opportunity to market a known seller, without excessive competition. This is most readily apparent when you move from one section of the country to another. In this circumstance, you have the advantage of a broader experience and more objectivity in identifying a market.

A strong warning is appropriate here! Remember, we said there were two essential ingredients for product selection. One is consumer demand and the other is your ability to

> **Our Experience**
>
> This is how we decided on a product line. In late 1984, we moved to Austin, Texas, from Eastern Tennessee. Susie was interested in country decorating and crafts and had sold handmade products in seasonal shows in Tennessee. Upon our arrival to Texas, she quickly discovered that there were only two small outlets for these products and these were confined to two major shopping malls. Austin was booming at the time and many people were moving in daily. Although the economy has since gone through several boom-and-bust cycles, the demand for our products has remained strong.

secure and market it successfully. Even though you have identified a product that is a proven seller and has not yet saturated the market, you will not be successful if you can't get it or if you don't have the talents, knowledge, and skills to market it. If we had not had Susie's skills and talents in selecting, displaying, and marketing country decorating accessories, we could not have succeeded!

Whether you're selling fertilizer or furniture, it's important that you know, understand, and are enthusiastic about the product and its uses and that you are able to relate this knowledge and enthusiasm to your customers. You may be able to get the training and knowledge from your suppliers, but only you can supply the enthusiasm and innate talents necessary to sell your product successfully.

I've mentioned the competitive environment, but the subject deserves a little more consideration. While it is important to move quickly to be on the cutting edge of a new product or trend, it is also important to consider the likelihood of future competition from "The Big Boys" and whether or not you can continue to compete successfully. For example, as we mentioned earlier, the home video market was originally dominated by "mom-and-pop" operators. But, once the popularity of the product became obvious, the field was taken over by giant stores operated by the large retailers, which have the advantage of strong financing and staying power.

It's a bit of a paradox, but a new product may be too hot, if it is likely to prove so popular that it attracts the interest of the industry giants. That's not to say you should not take advantage of the emerging product. After all, David slew Goliath, and there are other ways to compete than on price and volume. But you may wish to evaluate a more established, broader-based product line, as opposed to sinking your savings in a single, hot new item. Of course, if you have the financing, there's nothing to keep *you* from becoming the giant of a new industry! Don't automatically discard an opportunity to get in on the ground floor. Just evaluate the possibilities carefully.

As the fellow who quit his job grading potatoes said, "It's not the work, it's all those decisions!" The road to successful retailing is fraught with many critical decisions that only you can make, so it is important to analyze every aspect of each situation carefully. But, it's also important to make a decision promptly and proceed to the next one. Don't become paralyzed and fail to act!

Selling "Green"

Whether or not you believe in the theory of global warming, one cannot deny the increasing consciousness about the earth's environment on the part of many consumers. The environmental or "green" movement is not new. It began years ago and seems to be growing. Originally it was focused on clean water and air, saving the rain forests, and recycling. Today, much of the emphasis is on carbon dioxide emissions, and reducing our dependence on petroleum and its derivatives. Recent TV shows and news articles have shown how to calculate one's "carbon footprint," meaning the amount of carbon dioxide that is generated by one's activities. They also suggest means to reduce carbon use, or compensate for it, by planting trees, for example.

Without passing judgment on the correctness or practicality of the positions taken by the various groups involved on both sides of this issue, the green movement seems to be here to stay, and offers a market niche on which small retailers may wish to focus. This could be an entire store, or only parts of their product line. Catering to this market might be judged enlightened, or cynical, depending on which side of the issue you happen to fall, but it is definitely the stuff of which entrepreneurship is made. Obviously, your success in this area will vary according to the location of your store, and on the number of environmentally conscious consumers living in your area.

The "green" theme could be built into your store's daily operations, as an example of ways to reduce environmental impacts. Some examples are:

- Use natural light to minimize lighting requirements.
- Use solar panels for heating.
- Use recycled materials for your gift wrapping, and other paper products.
- Purchase wind power from your local power company if they offer it.
- Offer discounts to customers who demonstrate participation in local environmental projects, such as tree planting or building restoration.

You can also consider setting aside a section of your store where environmental products are grouped, with appropriate signage and display motifs. Some examples of products in this category are:

- Articles made from recycled products
- Handmade objects that support alternative income for indigent peoples who are otherwise cutting down rain forests to make a living
- Products with high energy efficiency ratings
- Products that reduce dependence on petroleum, such as bicycles and scooters

- Locally made products that reduce transportation costs and fuel use
- Products that can be returned to your store for recycling after use

Compatibility with Your Lifestyle

Some products carry with them limitations as to when, where, and how they can be successfully marketed. You should seriously consider whether these requirements are compatible with your own personal or family lifestyle preferences.

For example, you may decide that doughnuts would be a great product for your area. You should realize, however, that doughnuts are best sold between the hours of 5:00 A.M. and noon, which means you will need to be up every day at 1:00 or 2:00 A.M. in order to make them on time! Is that how you want to spend the next several years of your life? Other products may require outlets in undesirable, remote, or crowded locations. If you are uncomfortable in crowds, you might not want to sell magazines on a crowded street corner.

Sometimes, we overestimate our ability to adapt to adverse environments and glibly conclude that we can stand anything for the sake of a successful business.

A man I once knew was considering buying a dairy. For several days, he set his alarm for 3:00 A.M. and got up and dressed to try out the proposed hours. This may sound extreme, but if there is any doubt, you should actually live for several days under the conditions that you will be facing, perhaps by getting a job in someone else's store (make sure you do it in an area outside your target market so the store owner doesn't end up thinking you were spying on her operation!).

Can You Make a Profit?

Let's assume you've now identified a product or line of products for which a substantial demand exists and that is not flooding your market area. There's one final test: profitability. It doesn't matter if you can sell a thousand widgets a day if you can't buy and sell them at prices that will generate a reasonable profit margin. For example, you may be able to open a bait shop to sell worms at your local fishing lake. There's a big demand and there's not a lot of competition. You estimate you can sell 100 boxes of worms a day. However, they will cost you $1.50 a box and local fishermen are only willing to pay $2 a box for them. Rent and overhead will run about $30 a day, which means that your net profit of $20 a day is not sufficient to keep you in business, even though sales are good. Don't overlook profitability in your search for a product line.

Your choice of products to market has a decided effect on your expenses, your space requirements, your need for employ- ees (both number and degree of training), and the location you will need. If you choose to sell computers, for example, you will need to hire employees with specialized knowledge and training and you will probably need to provide customer training and software. This will make it more difficult to find and keep qualified employees and require you to provide a broader range of services than, say, an ice cream shop. However, you will require more help in an ice cream shop, and dealing with unskilled and younger employees carries its own set of problems.

Of course, you can always move in different directions with products after the store opens, provided the new products are com- patible with your location, space, etc. Although some diversification is healthy, we do caution you not to try to cover too much of the waterfront. You've heard the old saying, "jack of all trades, and mas- ter of none." You may wind up in that situation, if you try to include too great a variety of products and become known as a junk shop.

Obviously, trends and tastes come and go, so you have to stay up on current trends and move to other product lines when neces- sary. Your best strategy, however, is to stake out a reasonably well defined product line and stick to it, unless your market deterio- rates. You should bring in new products that are outside your gen- eral product area a few at a time, but only if they are compatible,

We were very careful about the kind and quality of merchandise that we brought into our shop. We were not a "high-end" gift shop, nor were we a dime store. We tried to target the middle-class consumer, including young couples and other upwardly mobile consumers. These groups may not have large current incomes, but they have specific tastes and desires and they have prospects for increasing their disposable income in the future. We tried to keep most items in the $5-to-$75 price range, while maintaining a good quality product that did not look mass-produced. We also stuck pretty closely to the country theme.

Our Experience

they are of good quality, and there is an expressed or perceived demand from current customers. Try bringing them in on a limited basis, allot them a small amount of space, and carefully gauge your customers' reactions.

In summary, your selected products should be:

◆ Products that you know and are enthusiastic about
◆ Products that are demonstrated sellers in areas similar to yours
◆ Products for which your market is not saturated
◆ Products that will generate sufficient profits to enable you to stay in business

It's a whole lot easier to write this list than for you to do it, but we know of no substitute for investing adequate time and energy in this selection process. Of such effort and persistence successful retailers are made!

Chapter 7

What Venue
Will You Use?

Prior to about 1990, this chapter would have been unnecessary. Up until then, starting a retail store meant only one thing: setting up shop in a storefront in a high-traffic area and selling to customers who walked through the front door. Today, there are other choices born out of the technological advances of the past two decades. In the past, a retailer had access to a market that consisted of those consumers within travel distance of his or her store location and within the reach of his or her advertising. Advances in communication and transportation, along with changes in consumer preferences and innovations in co-op marketing, have changed all that. Today, a retailer need not even have a static location. He or she can sell to markets around the world, literally, via the internet and catalogs, or sell through local or regional cooperative markets operated by someone else.

Retail venues can be grouped loosely under four categories: traditional fixed locations, cooperative stores, catalogs, and internet selling. Here is a brief overview of each.

Traditional Fixed Locations

This is still the most prevalent means of retailing and the main focus of this book. It requires the greatest amount of infrastructure and involves more intensive planning and structure than the other venues. The success of traditional retailing rests on the intersection of a consumer's needs with the products offered by a seller, at a particular place and time. Orchestrating this convergence of needs and offerings is what this book is all about. Most of the remaining chapters describe the steps necessary to achieve this objective.

Cooperative Markets

If you are unsure about opening a stand-alone retail store or lack the finances or time to do it, you might wish to consider becoming a tenant in one or more of the merchandise and antique malls or flea markets that have blossomed across the United States in recent years. In a cooperative market, you normally rent a booth and pay a fixed amount per square foot per month, in addition to a percentage of sales, usually 10 percent to 15 percent. Some of these markets are true co-ops, with each tenant working several hours a month in exchange for some of the rental fee.

Some of these markets maintain a high-quality sales environment; others are little more than organized garage sales. You will need to inspect prospective venues carefully, inquire about policies and payment procedures, and assure yourself that it is a legitimate going concern.

These markets have some advantages. Most will collect and pay sales taxes for you and the leases are generally short term, allowing you to close out if sales do not justify continuing. The financial requirements to start up are also lower than for a separate store.

Disadvantages include the facts that you are at the mercy of someone else's selling practices, sales volume is usually relatively low, and sale of your goods may be affected by the poor displays and housekeeping of adjacent booths.

If you are limited in the amount of cash you can invest and can be satisfied with a small income from sales or if you want to try out retailing on a small scale before striking out on your own, cooperative marketing may be the way to go.

Catalog Selling

Up until recently, only large retailers such as Sears, L.L. Bean, and Land's End had the resources to market goods via catalogs. Using catalogs to sell merchandise can still be an expensive proposition for the small retailer, although simpler, more economical methods for producing catalogs have put it within reach of many retailers, especially if they have a smaller array of products. Mailing lists can be purchased that target particular demographics or specific geographic areas.

Offsetting these lower costs are the generally higher mailing costs charged by the U.S. Postal Service, as it has attempted to reduce subsidies to mass mailers. These mailing costs are twofold, applying to mailing both catalogs and purchased merchandise. On the plus side, consumers have become accustomed to the convenience of shopping via catalogs and seem willing to accept paying shipping costs. Other issues associated with selling via catalogs are:

- Maintaining a toll-free telephone number to receive orders
- Operating a shipping and receiving facility
- Packaging and insurance expenses
- Maintaining convenient business hours often means a 24/7 operation
- Dealing with returns and complaints through the mail and over the telephone

Internet Selling

The last years of the previous millennium saw the meteoric rise of a new phenomenon in retailing: buying and selling merchandise on the world wide web. Stocks of the so-called dotcom companies rose, along with the belief that the internet was going to replace virtually everything we had used previously to communicate, advertise, sell, buy, educate our kids, engage in romance, spread our religious beliefs, and on and on. As the new millennium dawned, it turned out that, while the internet was indeed a major leap forward in some of our practices, such as email (and, sadly, pornography, sexual crimes against children, and the spreading of hate), it became clear that it had not lived up to its hype in many of the other areas.

As the reality dawned that most of the heralded dotcom commerce sites had not turned a single penny of profit after years of operation, investors began to retreat and the year 2000 saw a major fallout of internet companies that had depended on the constant infusion of new capital for operating funds. The search engine and internet news sites have been upstaged by social networking sites such a Twitter, Facebook, and Pinterest, all of which have a large marketing and advertising component.

Should You Become an E-Tailer?

Despite the bursting of the dotcom bubble, there is still growth in the amount of trade conducted over the internet. Shoppers are clearly gaining confidence in the security of using their credit cards for purchases from websites and seem enamored with the speed and convenience of internet shopping. Most major retail chains now have websites from which one can purchase all or a selection of their wares. Most of the web commerce sites deal in mass-produced goods that are commonly found in Walmarts and other mainline department and discount specialty stores. However, the ability to quickly access information and find specific items on the internet using rapidly advancing search engines has contributed to the rise of more and more specialized retail sites.

This opens the possibility of marketing your products to a worldwide market, with minimal investment, and you should consider the internet as a primary selling venue or, at least, as an adjunct to other retail venues.

Of course, internet selling has its own set of problems and logistics issues that you must consider.

Recently, however, more and more "mom-and-pop" sites have appeared on the internet, reflecting the increasing ease and decreasing costs associated with an internet presence. These sites offer virtually anything you wish to buy, but many have not been effective in attracting substantial clienteles, because either the websites are poorly designed or they fail to gain recognition from the major search engines.

Elsewhere in this book the position of the small retailer was compared with the giant big box retailers, with a warning that you cannot hope to compete with the big boys on their own turf. Rather, you should compete on other terms. Does that mean that you should ignore the possibilities of internet marketing? Well, yes and no. While the large stores that simply use the web to sell the same old merchandise haven't really changed the equation with respect to you, the small retailer, there are some new entries on the web that attempt to eliminate the advantages you have. These advantages are the provision of outstanding service and the marketing of unique and one-of-a-kind merchandise.

While this new breed of ecommerce sites still cannot match your ability to serve your customers in a personal way, some of them will offer some serious competition. I refer to sites such as eBay, which serve as "flea markets" on the web. From your computer, you can browse through an almost unlimited array of unique items, including memorabilia, antiques, and collectibles, as well as more conventional merchandise, look at color photos, and then haggle on the purchase price. These sites have attracted a lot of attention, due in part to the novelty and challenge of bidding for items against other unknown potential buyers. Other small retailers are also becoming active through their own websites.

Given this situation, it seems prudent to at least investigate the feasibility of getting your store into the ether. How do you go about this seemingly daunting task? Not surprisingly, the best source of information about ecommerce is the internet itself. Simply log on to one of the search engine sites (I like Google.com) and type in key words such as "ecommerce" or "online retailing" and you will be led to more information than you ever wanted. To help you find your way through the maze, let's take it step by step.

The first thing to consider is whether or not you want to alter or expand your business to accommodate the requirements of ecommerce. Using the internet for selling means that you must essentially go into the mail order business. That means warehousing inventory and setting up a shipping facility. It also means that your contact with customers will not be face to face, but through electronic mail, regular mail, and telephone.

Our Experience ● One of the main reasons we opted to go into retail in the first place was the people factor—getting to meet new people, interact with them, and form new personal relationships. For that reason, we considered ecommerce several times and decided against it. It remains an option that must be considered, since remaining economically viable is the ultimate necessity for any retailer. But, if you are a consummate "people person," then you may not be happy as an e-tailer.

Another threshold question that must be answered involves the logistics and facilities involved. Do you have storage and shipping space available or can you obtain it at a reasonable cost? Retail sales space is costly and it usually does not pay to use much of it for storage. One solution to the space problem is to lease less costly space, but that usually means at a different location, meaning that you will have to hire additional staff to run the shipping operation or you will have to burn the candle on both ends (and maybe in the middle) to commute between the sites and still get all your work done. Remember: customers of mail order houses have been wooed away from conventional shopping with promises of prompt shipping and you cannot afford to let orders lie around unfulfilled for too long. So, are you willing to work harder, split up your work sites, or hire additional employees who may have to work without your personal supervision? If the answer is yes, then you should proceed to the next step.

Starting Out

How do I get on the web? Fortunately, there are many options, ranging from listing a few items on an existing site such as eBay, to establishing your own full-service website to sell the complete line of goods that you carry in your own store. Let's take a look at the options one at a time.

Recently, intermediary sites have appeared in many communities, offering to market your products on eBay. They charge a fee, of course, but they allow a person with no interest or skills in the internet to participate in the auction.

If you opt for the low-end solution of listing with an auction site, your initial investment will be virtually nothing. One of our friends currently uses eBay to market a small number of antiques and collectibles. The advantages of this option are the lack of front-end costs and you don't have to get a website or be set up for credit card payments over the internet. The auction sites handle all the details for you for a small fee. Disadvantages are that you cannot market for a fixed price, but must settle for the high bid, you still have risk if a high bidder reneges, and you are responsible for packing and shipping. The logistics of getting a large number of items on these sites are considerable and tend to limit your product line and therefore your profits. Jacquelyn Lynn has published a detailed, step-by-step manual for starting an eBay business, *Start Your Own Business on eBay* (Entrepreneur Press).

The next option is listing with a major dotcom reseller, such as Yahoo. Yahoo offers something called "Yahoo Store" that includes all the tools for setting up your own website and handling all the credit card transactions, using secure software. The cost for a professional-level store with complete online support and advanced features can cost as little as $35 per month. Advantages of this option are that you will have instant listing on the hosting search engine and the cost will be low.

Another reselling option is a catalog website that hosts a number of smaller retailers that will let you post your goods on their site for a fee. They typically handle all the logistics for you. The disadvantages of this approach are that you are tied to one of the major dotcoms and their marketing and search engines and you must be fairly proficient in using computers and web software to effectively use all the tools and services offered.

The third and most costly option is the development and operation of your own ecommerce site. Whether or not you decide to pursue a full-blown ecommerce site, it is essential in today's world, to have a website for advertising your store and its products, and to accommodate the customer communications that we discuss in a later chapter. Today, setting up a simple website is relatively easy, using the tools supplied by your internet service provider, with perhaps some help from a family member or local technical service freelancer. The details of obtaining a domain name are discussed below.

Unless you are willing to become an accomplished HTML programmer and website designer, you will need professional assistance in order to launch a comprehensive ecommerce retail site. There are several things you must do.

♦ Obtain a domain name.
♦ Design a website.
♦ Develop and customize your sales.
♦ Get your credit card processing system in place.
♦ Locate your site on the major search engines.
♦ Open your "virtual store."

Assistance in all of these areas is readily available. It comes in varying degrees of comprehensiveness and expense, and can be found by typing "internet retailing" or similar key words in one of the internet search engines such as Yahoo or Google. You will be shown a plethora of sites offering to help you set up your online retail store, for a fee.

Domain Names

A domain name is the address that the internet uses to uniquely identify your site on the world wide web. For example, "Yahoo. com" is a domain.

The Internet Corporation for Assigned Names and Numbers (ICANN) exists to maintain the domain names and numbers system. It uses independent registrars who actually submit the technical information to ICANN for registration. These registrars often have brokers who work through them to register names.

Although theoretically anyone can register a domain, the practical reality is that many of the best names have been given out.

Many are held by registrars and brokers who registered large numbers of domain names in the hope of reselling them. For example, a recent check for the domain name greatgiftsforyou.com revealed that it was available for resale for about $900. Domain names are available for terms ranging from one to ten years, for a fee ranging from $3 to $10,000 or more. There are many companies on the internet that will register your name for a small fee. Most website designers or hosts will register your domain name as part of their services. I recommend using their services and letting them go through the process of getting your preferred name registered.

Website Design and Hosting

There are also many companies on the internet that will host your website. This means they will provide the server and storage area for your site on their own hardware, so that you will not have to use your own computer's hard drive. This option of using a host is the most practical one for most small retailers; I recommend it if you choose to enter the realm of ecommerce. These companies will design your website to your specifications and most will offer templates to accommodate your needs, in attractive formats and colors and with animation. Typically this does not involve reinventing the wheel, as there are many models available that can be customized to suit your needs.

Website design is a highly competitive business, with companies offering a full range of services for very low prices. Website design with a "shopping cart" can range between $500 to $5,000, or more. However, many companies advertising on the internet offer package deals for registering your domain, designing your website, installing a shopping cart software system, and setting up secure online payment processing for as low as $10 per month, plus processing fees in the neighborhood of 2.5 percent of sales and $0.30 per transaction. The prices go up as the number of items increases and the sophistication of the item listing increases, for example with more pictures, animation, and graphics. Most of the sales software also offers statistical analysis of sales that can help you plan for new products and target your advertising. As with all internet advertising, *caveat emptor* applies, so be sure to ask for references and check out companies that offer deals too good to be true. They probably are!

Credit Card Processing

If you do not enter into a package deal with a site host, you will need to have a credit card processing agreement with a bank and/or a processing company. Many times the bank will offer a combined package. Processors will typically charge a discount fee of 1.5 to 3 percent and a transaction fee of $.10 to $.25 for each transaction. If you already have an agreement for your retail store, you may be able to use the same processor to handle your ecommerce transactions.

Sam's Club offers credit card processing services to small retailers as part of their merchant services. PayPal, initially started by eBay is also an option for online payments.

Reaching Potential Buyers

No matter how attractive and comprehensive your website, it will do you no good unless it is accessible to a large number of potential buyers. Unless you can get on the major search engines, you will likely not reach a large market. Since different search engines follow different procedures, you should probably seek assistance from your website designer and host in getting your site listed. Some search engines will list you for a fee; you may want to consider doing it to ensure immediate exposure or you might want to delay broad exposure until you are more comfortable with your internet presence.

Shipping and Receiving

Regardless of the option chosen, you must also be set up to pack and ship orders promptly. Customers who use mail order are accustomed to prompt delivery, especially before Christmas and other major holidays. To meet these expectations, you will need to have regular pickups from UPS, FedEx, and perhaps other parcel shippers. These shipping costs can be substantial, especially over-night or two-day air shipping. Of course, you will need a supply of shipping materials, such as different sizes of boxes, packing peanuts, bubble wrap, tape, etc. The prices of these materials, while not overwhelming, can add significantly to your costs. These costs can either be factored into your selling price or added as a separate shipping charge. Since many ecommerce sites offer free shipping as incentives, you might elect to include the shipping charges in the selling price. If you do this, you should monitor shipping costs carefully to ensure that you recover your full costs.

Sales Tax

Another issue you must face is sales tax collection. Many states are now enacting laws to collect sales taxes on goods delivered in their states from other states. This could require you to collect and remit taxes to a large number of states; however, there are several national legislative initiatives to deal with this issue at the federal level. The outcome of these proposed legislative changes will either minimize restrictions or increase them, depending on which point of view prevails.

Evaluate Your Options

So, the decision, as always, is yours. My personal opinion is that, while commerce on the internet will undoubtedly increase, there will always be a place for the local retailer who maintains an attractive shop and offers specialty merchandise and personal service to customers. Humans are innately social and will always seek the company of others, even in buying and selling goods. One reason that telecommuting (working at home via computers) has not grown more rapidly is the feeling of isolation due to lack of social contact with co-workers experienced while working at home. Therefore, I believe there will always be many people who will want to see and feel items before they buy them and retail stores will remain. My suggestion is that you answer the following questions to determine if e-tailing is for you and, if so, what levels are appropriate to pursue.

- Is your business suffering from competition on the internet? Have customers asked if you have a web page?
- Are products identical to the ones you sell available readily on the internet? Be sure to check!
- Do you have the desire and resources to run a packing and shipping operation?
- Are you turned off by the impersonality of anonymous selling?
- Do you have the space to store merchandise for shipping to customers?
- Can you generate enough revenue to justify hiring and training the employees necessary to run the shipping operation? Some research into similar businesses should give you some idea.
- Will the profits generated justify the upfront and continuing maintenance costs? Prepare a simple business plan to estimate results.
- Are your computer skills good enough to allow you to do most of the work on your ecommerce development?
- Should you go with a limited site tied to an existing web business or search engine or should you set up an independent site? Check with a web hosting company for more information.

Perhaps you can manage both your "real" and "virtual" stores and profit from both. Or, you may opt to stay exclusively with one or the other. Either way, the choice depends on your own inclinations, the availability of space and staffing, and that all-important item—profit.

This chapter is intended to give only a cursory treatment to alternative venues for retailing. Other resources are listed in Appendices B and D. The remainder of this book will focus on traditional retailing. Even if you choose traditional retailing, you should consider the use of one or more of the alternative venues as adjuncts to your main business. You may find that you can greatly enhance your profitability by expanding your scope to include alternative means of reaching customers.

Chapter 8

How Will You
Choose a Location?

W e've all heard—and gotten tired of—that old realtor's cliché that the three important aspects of real estate are location, location, and location. While location is a very important part of the retail business, it may not always be crucial in determining success or failure.

Our Experience ● Due to the extreme shortage of retail space at the time we went into business, we were forced to locate in a somewhat remote strip center at the edge of town. In spite of this marginal location, we were able to build a loyal clientele based on our product, and word-of-mouth publicity with minimal advertising. We later relocated this first store to a strip center at a major intersection where there is a major chain supermarket. This relocation did result in increased sales of from 10 to 20 percent, thus validating the importance of location. However, we were able to relocate during a depressed rental market, at a reduced rent. Often this is not the case, so the increased sales volume of a better location may be partially or totally offset by increased costs. This is especially true of some major shopping mall locations, where rents can be exorbitant.

When we opened our second store, we opted for a location in an upscale strip center with mostly national chain tenants.

Our Experience ● While the new store's sales consistently exceeded the first store's, we found that the premium rents in the second center gradually ate away at our profits. By the time we decided to close it, the rapidly escalating rents had virtually erased the advantages from the increase in sales. Another reason for closing was that we were advised by the center's manager that they were targeting national chains and that they really did not want individually owned stores.

Selecting a General Location

In today's mobile society, consideration of location can involve a truly global search. Although a business can be established successfully in the place where you have lived all your life, it seems that the growth of entrepreneurship is at least partly the result of the exposure of more and more people to different areas and cultures. In our own case, we have lived in eight places in the United States and, as a result, have had the opportunity to see successes and failures of many different types of businesses in varied settings.

Our point is not that you have to be a world traveler to establish a successful business, but that there are hundreds of choices for locating a business, largely because of the mobility of our society. Exposure to different places and cultures can sometimes give you the edge in spotting a product or service that will be successful.

So, if the world is your oyster, how do you go about narrowing it down? I suggest you select your location from the outside in, so to speak, based on your own particular circumstances, needs, and personal preferences. That is, decide on a country, state, region, city neighborhood, and street address, in that order.

While it is entirely possible to establish businesses in other countries, we will assume that you are likely to choose a location within your own country, although the principles involved in locating in another country will be the same. You will probably choose your present location, simply because you are there and are familiar with the economy and the area. Or, you may be looking to return to the place of your roots, possibly after retiring, to establish a business among your childhood friends and families. Then again, you may simply want to move to a new area to be near children and grandchildren, escape the cold or heat, live in the mountains or on the beach, or for a score of other personal reasons.

Whatever the reasons for choosing a location with which you are not currently familiar, it is imperative that you spend some time in the new location to become oriented. Notice I said, "currently familiar." Many of us assume we know the place where we grew up, even though we have been gone many years. People and places change, so, before you decide to open a toy store in your old neighborhood, better check to be sure the neighborhood still has kids, rather than senior citizens. There are other, subtler changes that occur that can have an impact on your business. The people who used to love ice cream and hot dogs may now be on a low-cholesterol, low-fat diet. Or, conversely, they may still thrive on traditional foods, while the rest of the world is on a health kick.

Personal and Family Lifestyle Issues

You should get familiar with the proposed location of your new business and determine if you can be content and happy there, given your personal lifestyle preferences. If you don't live there, visit and spend time with the people and get to know their wants and needs. You may be able to spend your vacation in the area or, preferably, several shorter periods at different times of the year. You should try to determine if you would be happy living there. If you are not content, your business will suffer. Many are the people who have returned to their hometown only to find they didn't fit in anymore. Remember Thomas Wolfe's assertion, "You can't go home again!" It's also possible that the weather that seemed pleasantly warm from your vantage point in the Snow Belt is actually miserably hot, once you get there. Don't ignore your own personal lifestyle needs in choosing a business location. Many of the hot spots for new retail opportunity are in resort areas or in new or restored downtown "festive retail" centers designed to cater to the convention or tourist trade. These are opposites in the rural/urban spectrum and you will need to evaluate your environmental desires in this regard. Many of these situations are also seasonal, with short, frantically busy periods, followed by the doldrums. Does this pattern fit in with your vision of your preferred lifestyle? Can you handle the pressure of the peak selling season and, perhaps just as importantly, can you handle the periods of inactivity and boredom?

Narrowing the Field

Once you have chosen a state, region, and city, it's time to focus on the specific neighborhood in which you will locate. This will involve more detailed and objective criteria, as opposed to the more general and subjective process of choosing an area in which to live.

One of the keys to retail success is traffic, both vehicular and pedestrian. While you can survive on a good vehicular location alone if you have a good product mix, it is much better to have significant walk-by traffic, also.

The first step is to identify those streets and highways that carry large traffic volumes. You can get this information for free or a nominal copying charge from your city traffic engineering department or the state highway department. Also, chambers of commerce often have this data available. Get a city or area map and pencil in the high-traffic corridors. Then, get in your car and drive these corridors, noting any especially favorable or unfavorable locations. This should enable you to stake out the general areas that seem most favorable for your shop location. Having identified potential high-traffic corridors, evaluate them using the following criteria:

Proximity to large groups of potential customers. A high-traffic highway may not be a good location if it is simply a conduit between two distant inhabited areas.

General availability of space for retailing. Knowing a good location doesn't do you any good if you can't locate there.

Customer income level. By this time, you should know what your product line and price range will be, so it's important to match it with an appropriate customer base. You wouldn't want to locate a fur salon in a neighborhood of factory workers or a bait shop in an area of high-dollar condos. Common sense should serve you well here. Another factor here is disposable income. A store selling discretionary items may not do well in an area of high incomes if everyone is mortgaged to the hilt and has little disposable income. This is not easy to evaluate. Your best bets for this information are shopping center demographic material, your chamber of commerce, and knowledge you gain from actually living in an area. The U.S. Census Bureau has some helpful data, but it may be as much as ten years old near the end of a decade. Census demographic data can be accessed via the internet at www.census.gov.

Proximity to competitors. While locating near competitors can be advantageous in some situations, such as resort and "theme" areas, moving next door to an established direct competitor is not usually a great idea. Some overlapping of product lines is OK and can produce a synergistic effect; some businesses, such as auto dealers and furniture stores, now purposely locate together to profit from a larger customer pool.

Your own convenience. This is an important consideration, since one of the reasons for starting a store is to improve your

Our Experience

In our decision to locate a store, the commute weighed heavily. Since Susie was to run the store, she decided it was important to be relatively close to home to avoid long drive times through heavy traffic. Also, we had some knowledge of income levels and disposable income in our part of town, which was growing rapidly at the time, ensuring a supply of new potential customers—or so we thought. In actuality, the economy in our city went bust about two years after we opened and the stream of in-migration turned to out-migration, almost overnight. This could have proven fatal to our business if we had not been located on a major traffic artery, and if we had not built up a loyal customer following before the downturn. Also, shortly after we signed the lease, we discovered that our street was scheduled to be widened and rebuilt. Fortunately, we were able to complete our lease term and relocate before the work began.

lifestyle and get out of the rat race. If you wind up fighting traffic morning and night or you have to work in an unsafe or undesirable area of town, you might not be any better off. Flexibility in your point of residence can be a factor here.

As our story in the sidebar shows, it is absolute folly to assume that things will stay as they are. Our economy is driven by forces that, I am convinced, have not even begun to be understood by economic experts, let alone amateurs such as you and me. So, expect the unexpected, be flexible, and be prepared to roll with the punches, because you will take some hits. Learn from our experience: Always check with your local roadway officials before locating, since a major project can disrupt traffic for years and sound the death knell for a small business.

The second reason for mentioning this abrupt economic reversal is to emphasize that you can survive in adversity if you do not put all your eggs into one basket, from a location perspective. Try to choose a place that has high traffic volumes and a substantial resident population nearby.

Let's assume now that you have narrowed the general location down to a specific area within which you can search for just the right site for your shop. Now, it is time to get even more specific. I'll give you some tips on finding that perfect location!

Zeroing In

Once you've identified the general area, it's time to get down to the detail work of finding an affordable location that will provide you an attractive place to transform your inventory into sales and, more importantly, profits! Important considerations in selecting a site are:

♦ Zoning compatibility
♦ Compatibility with neighboring merchants
♦ Special "atmosphere" requirements
♦ Space requirements
♦ Cost of space and landlord rules
♦ Customer traffic

Let's take them one by one.

Zoning Compatibility

Visit your local zoning authority and obtain zoning maps and a list of allowable uses in each zoning category. Explain to the zoning official what you will be selling, in detail, and obtain, preferably in writing, the zones in which you are allowed to operate. Zoning is usually handled by the planning department in most cities.

If this seems like a waste of time, let me assure you that I have direct knowledge of cases where business plans and even operating businesses have been ruined by running afoul of these laws. It doesn't matter that another business has operated there for years, since most zoning law provisions are invoked only when someone complains. Many older businesses are also "grandfathered" until they cease operating, by virtue of having already been there when the laws were passed or changed. All it takes is a disgruntled neighbor to shut you down, if you haven't checked carefully. There is no need to be called out on a technicality, when there are so many fun ways to go broke on your own!

If the perfect location for your shop does not have the proper zoning, all is not necessarily lost. All cities have provisions for rezoning property. In some jurisdictions, this is a straightforward and simple process, but in most places it involves a complicated, time-consuming, and expensive ordeal. It can also become emotional and very unpleasant if the neighborhood chooses to oppose it. Under these circumstances, you may win the zoning battle but lose your clientele through alienation. Unless the process is simple and you will have no opposition, our advice is to skip it and find another space. Hell hath no fury like neighbors who believe your business will lower their property values or interfere with their way of life!

Merchants

Next, you should consider compatibility with other shops in your potential location. By this, I don't mean whether you have the same astrological sign, race, or religion as the other shop owners, but whether or not you will be able to share, to some extent, the customer base of your neighbors.

Our Experience ● Our first two shops were located in midsized retail strip centers that also contained supermarkets, family haircutting shops, restaurants, a pool chemical store, dry cleaners, a dentist, a national chain retailer, a frozen yogurt shop, and assorted other general retail shops plus several empty spaces. The customers of the other businesses in the centers were also potentially our customers to some degree, although some of them, such as the pool supply store, catered mainly to men, while our primary customers were women. Our third store was located behind our residence, in a separate building. We operated a bed-and-breakfast in our historic home in a mixed-use section of town. The gift shop fit in well with this endeavor, but walk-in traffic was essentially nil.

There are some situations of which you should be wary. If you are planning a religious bookstore, for example, you probably should steer clear of a center filled mostly with businesses selling liquor, adult books, sexual paraphernalia, and other products and services not generally directed at the church-going crowd. That's an extreme example, but I think you get the picture. More typical examples might include locating a computer store in an antique mall, or a candy store next to a gym and weight loss studio. There is also the question of whether or not to locate in the same center or area with a shop in the same generic business. For example, if you plan a gift shop, should you locate in a shopping center with another gift shop? It probably depends more on the specific product lines, styles, and orientation than on the generic name.

Our first shop carried gifts, decorating accessories, furniture, cards, and other items that were mostly handmade in the "country" motif. There is virtually no overlap with a typical greeting card shop, which also carries gifts, but in a different decorating style. In fact, locating together could actually result in increased sales for both shops by attracting a larger customer pool that may be interested in both lines of products. This is, in fact, what we found in one shopping center where we were considering locating. However, we were not successful in convincing the other shop owners that we would not diminish their sales and we were forced to look elsewhere.

Most shopping centers have agreements not to lease space to a competing business and the current tenants may be able to exclude you. You may be able to avoid being blackballed by visiting with potential competitors and agreeing not to compete directly on main product lines. Even though this makes sense to you, don't assume the other shop owners will agree.

Special Atmosphere Requirements

Sometimes a product line requires a special atmosphere in which to be displayed, which can affect your choice of locations, although there are ways to overcome this factor through innovative displays, as we will discuss in more detail in a later chapter.

Given a choice between location and atmosphere, I would almost always choose location, since a perfect atmosphere won't be enough if you can't get people there. But, to the extent possible, it makes sense to consider this alternative. Although this may not always be possible, try to get your lessor to agree not to rent adjacent spaces to a business that would destroy your atmosphere. Your rental library business may not flourish next to a bowling alley. Most lessors are sensitive to these situations and try to accommodate reasonable requests. Anyway, it doesn't hurt to ask.

> **Our Experience**
>
> Since we wanted to open a country gift and decorative accessories shop, our first choice was an old historic house that would be compatible with our products and facilitate displaying them. Unfortunately, we could not find such a place in the area we had targeted as our market area, so we chose location over atmosphere and created our own "old house" atmosphere.

Space Needs

How much space do you need? This varies considerably, based on the kind of store, its location, and the cost of the space.

If you choose a high-dollar location such as a mall, you may wish to reduce the space somewhat, use virtually all of it for sales, and rent storage space at a cheaper location. This will save

Our Experience ● For our first gift shop, we started with 1,000 square feet, of which about 300 was devoted to storage, workspace, and a restroom, with the remainder in sales area. This proved to be about right, to start with, since our funds for inventory purchases were limited. We later expanded to 1,500 square feet in the first store, with 1,250 devoted to sales space and 250 in storage, restroom, etc. Our second store began with 1,200 square feet, which we later expanded to 1,400.

some overhead, but it will be a hassle to shuttle merchandise back and forth. You will need to plan your stocking carefully.

Chapter 10 gives some rules of thumb for estimating inventory costs per square foot. Using these and other data for your particular merchandise line, you can determine approximately how much space you can afford, initially. You should also try several possible store layouts on graph paper to see if the space will lend itself to an attractive and functional selling area. The shape and orientation of the space can be a substantial factor in its usefulness for your particular purpose. A long narrow space may give enough total area, but be unsuitable for display and traffic flow. On

Our Experience ● Because our second store rent was very high, we rented a mini-storage warehouse to house off-season merchandise and displays. We did not, however, store current stock in the warehouse.

the other hand, a square space may not permit you to divide up the area into room settings if your display scheme requires it.

A space about two or three times as deep as it is wide provides a very workable framework for most merchandise displays. If you are going into a new center, you can generally choose as much or as little width as you need, but the depth is normally fixed by the overall depth of the building. The width is determined by partitions, which are not usually constructed until the space is leased. The Americans with Disabilities Act and local codes also imposes certain requirements for access and restrooms that you must consider in laying out your space.

Costs and Landlord Rules

A new business needs to keep its overhead down. Your biggest single expense will almost surely be your rent. Therefore, it is appropriate to pay a lot of attention to this item—not to the exclusion of all else, particularly location, but a lot of attention is definitely justified. You also should be concerned about how the lessor's rules will impact your business and you personally.

There are four basic cost and rules categories for retail space. In ascending order of cost and degree of restrictions, they are:

- Your own home
- A detached house or other older structure
- A retail strip center
- A shopping mall

Unless you plan a very modest business, are located unusually, and don't mind people trampling through your domicile, your home is out, so we won't spend time dealing with this option. It is cheap, however, and might do the job in very unusual circumstances, especially for a retail business based in internet and catalog selling.

We've already discussed the separate house option to some extent. A converted residence or other freestanding structure may be a viable option for some businesses in some locations and should be thoroughly explored. If it is isolated from other businesses, you lose some traffic potential. But the reduced cost could offset this, and if the savings are invested in advertising, it could actually result in greater profits. Since you will likely be dealing with an individual owner, you may achieve a lower rent, but you may also end up with

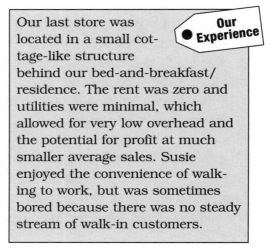

Our last store was located in a small cottage-like structure behind our bed-and-breakfast/residence. The rent was zero and utilities were minimal, which allowed for very low overhead and the potential for profit at much smaller average sales. Susie enjoyed the convenience of walking to work, but was sometimes bored because there was no steady stream of walk-in customers.

little maintenance and difficulty in getting repairs completed in a timely manner. You should have few, if any, rules with which to deal. A disadvantage will be that you usually must accept the space in its present configuration, which will limit your options for display. Look at the possibilities and see if any will work for you.

The retail strip center is the next most expensive space potential and, as you might expect, has its own set of pros and cons. While generally more expensive than the options discussed above, it will almost always bring you into contact with more potential customers. However, you are likely to have more rules and regulations. Strip centers usually have professional managers who can provide better maintenance and repair and who sometimes provide newsletters and group advertising opportunities for tenants. They also generally have structured lease provisions and little flexibility in dealing with you.

Many strip centers are managed by large national companies, which provide very good maintenance and upkeep of the center property. However, you likely will have a lot of rules and a lease that is long and detailed, most of the provisions of which were written to protect—guess who? That's right, the center owner! Most centers also have rules about signs, sidewalk displays, etc., most of which are for the general good of the tenants, but that are restrictive, nonetheless.

In bad economic times, these centers are not immune to financial problems and are prone to bankruptcy, resulting in management and ownership changes that affect the centers' viability. If you decide to locate in a strip center, try to choose one with a national or regional manager with a reputation for stability.

The ultimate location is that American icon, the shopping mall. These are the most expensive and restrictive. Most have rigid requirements for tenants regarding days and hours of operation, contributions to mall advertising campaigns, deliveries, etc. If you want to retain total independence in the operation of your business, the mall may not be for you. However, malls usually produce the highest sales volume, although not necessarily the highest profits, given the premium rental rates demanded.

One disadvantage of a mall location is in deliveries, if you have bulky items to sell, as malls usually have restricted access for vendors and the same problems for customers leaving with merchandise. Unless you are an anchor tenant, like Sears or JCPenney, you are unlikely to have direct sidewalk access. For some businesses, however, malls are the best place to be and should be strongly considered.

> **Our Experience**
>
> We rejected the shopping mall option, initially, because of the rules and because we wanted to cut our teeth in a less fast-paced environment.

Customer Traffic

The last factor is customer traffic. This is really not a stand-alone item, since it is interrelated with the other factors. It must be kept in mind, however, since it may be the most important factor to the success of your business. You may have the best-shaped, lowest-cost, best-located space in town, but if you don't have a substantial number of customers for your type of merchandise coming by your store, it will profit you little. To ensure this, you will have to observe and research the kinds of customers who typically come to the particular shopping area you choose. Most retail centers have a package of demographics that they will provide you. If they don't offer it, ask them for it. These packages typically contain information on the number, average income, and makeup of households within a one-mile and a five-mile radius. They will tell you, for example, how many households are single or married couples, whether they have children, and the range of ages of the residents. Spend some time analyzing

> **Our Experience**
>
> In our case, we wanted couples, preferably homeowners, with disposable incomes that would allow them to purchase gifts, furniture, and decorating accessories for their homes or for their friends and families. Our preferred age was between 20 and 55.

this data to see if the current customer base contains the kinds of people who are likely to buy your products.

Your product line might be better received by a particular group of customers. If you are selling ultra-modern furniture, for example, it probably wouldn't be a good idea to locate in a center surrounded by historic homes. It will take a little digging, but a thorough perusal of the demographic data can yield valuable insights into your potential customer pool.

Final Evaluation

You should know by now that a perfect location probably doesn't exist. You must evaluate all the options available to you, consider all the advantages and disadvantages of each, then choose the one that provides you with the advantages you consider most important. Take the process to the next step of negotiating a lease for a specific space. Chapter 9 focuses on this aspect.

Closing on Your Location

Buying vs. Leasing

The first decision you must make, after selecting a specific location, is whether to buy a building or lease space. If you choose a shopping center or mall, buying will not be an option and you will need to proceed to lease negotiation. If you have selected a stand-alone building or house, you may have the option to buy instead of lease. Let's look at the advantages of buying:

- ◆ You will build equity in real estate instead of enriching the owner by paying rent.
- ◆ You will have more control over finishing out and modifying your space.
- ◆ Mortgage payments may be lower than lease payments, depending on economic conditions and your credit rating.
- ◆ You will have more flexibility in exterior advertising and signage, and be able to match the overall appearance of your store to your desired theme.

As with almost everything, there are also disadvantages:

- ◆ You will have to use substantial amounts of your available cash to purchase or make a down payment on a building.

- ◆ You will have to secure insurance and utilities on your own.
- ◆ You will not be able to close or move your business as readily as with a short-term lease.
- ◆ You will be totally responsible for maintenance and security of your building and grounds.

If you elect to buy, the transaction will likely be a routine real estate purchase transaction that you can handle in much the same way as purchasing a home. There are many books on purchasing commercial real estate; your real estate or business broker will be a good source of information as well.

Negotiating the Lease

For most people entering into a new business for the first time, leasing space is likely to be the most favorable alternative, largely because of the need to conserve limited startup cash for use in paying for one-time costs and for purchasing initial inventory.

Negotiating a lease can be as simple as buying a toothbrush or as complicated and distasteful as buying a new car, complete with the playing of "The Game" to settle on a final price. Obviously, it's simpler if you're dealing with an individual owner who is very flexible or a large corporation whose policies allow for no negotiations. The results can be very different in these two extreme cases, but it can be very simple, as in "take it or leave it."

We'll assume that you will be dealing with a leasing agent or a shopping center manager and that there will

Our Experience ● Our first lease in a small, relatively remote strip center offered us very little room for negotiation on price because of a booming economy and an extreme shortage of retail space. We were, however, able to secure some concessions on the lease terms, as recommended by our attorney. Our second lease was negotiated in a lean economy, with retail space going begging, and we were able to gain major concessions on price, although the major national firm we were dealing with had standard lease agreement terms with which it was somewhat inflexible.

be some room for negotiation, as this is usually the case. The amount of leverage you have will vary greatly with the economy and the retail vacancy rate in your area.

You should, by all means, have an attorney review your first lease, but don't let him or her make your decisions. Attorneys are paid to point out potential risks and they may be overly cautious in trying to make sure you don't later blame them for failing to warn you properly. Listen to the attorney's advice and consider it, but don't be dominated by him or her. Make your own business decision, even if it does carry some risks. Remember: Life is uncertain. That's why I always eat dessert first!

Basic Lease Elements

Leases for retail space usually have minimum terms of three years, although shorter and longer terms are sometimes possible. The following are usually included in retail space leases, in various combinations.

- ◆ **A basic term.** The lessee—that's you—is obligated to pay for the space for a specific time period (usually three years), whether or not your business survives that long.
- ◆ **A basic rental rate.** This is calculated per square foot or as a percentage of gross sales, whichever is greater. Typical rents may range from $.90 to $3 per square foot per month or 6 percent of gross sales, whichever is greater.
- ◆ **Assignment of maintenance responsibility.** The lessee is normally responsible for maintaining all equipment serving his or her space, including electrical, plumbing, heating, air conditioning, and structural components. This may sound illogical, but it seems to be standard.
- ◆ **Water and sewer.** These are usually included in the lease rate, but expect to pay extra for gas, electricity, and trash removal.
- ◆ **Triple net.** This is a monthly charge, usually for the expense trio of taxes, insurance, and common area maintenance, hence the term "triple net." This charge is designed to allow the lessor to pass on his or her variable costs to you. They are normally

adjusted annually and can represent an additional 10 percent to 35 percent added to your basic rent.

- **Finish-out allowance.** In return for the three-year term of the lease, the lessor will usually provide you an allowance to finish out the space to your specifications. This is typically in the range of $10 to $30 per square foot, which is sufficient for basic walls, ceiling, lighting, electrical, plumbing, heating, air conditioning, and insulation. It does not normally cover wall finishes, carpet and floor tile, signs, and any other custom work to suit your shop's specific needs. The finish-out allowance amount and coverage are subject to negotiation, within a fairly narrow range.
- **Prepaid rent.** This is typically one to three months.
- **Security deposit.** This is usually zero to two months' rent.

As the first step in lease negotiations, contact leasing agents for spaces in which you are interested and ask for proposals. After receiving several, you should have an idea of the menu of terms and prices you will have to deal with in your negotiations. At this point, you may find it desirable to engage a leasing agent to negotiate the lease for you, if you feel overwhelmed by the task or if you are not a particularly good negotiator. You can do it yourself, however, and by following some basic guidelines, you should be able to achieve reasonable terms.

It will help if you can locate at least two spaces that can meet your needs, thus ensuring competition for your lease. Try to avoid getting emotionally attached to a particular space or location. It's easy to home in on it to the exclusion of all other possibilities, thus limiting your ability to secure favorable lease terms. If you have your heart set on a particular space, the lessor will probably sense it and try to drive a hard bargain.

After you receive the proposals from the leasing agents or center managers, don't let them pressure you into signing a lease prematurely. We suggest you prepare and submit a counter-offer, in writing, in response to the proposals. Some proposals you might consider including are:

- Lower basic rates
- No payment of percentage of sales or a smaller percentage
- Larger finish-out allowance and coverage of more improvements, such as floor coverings and interior partitions
- Graduated lease rates, starting low, but increasing over the lease term
- Limits on "triple net" charges
- Inclusion of some utilities in the base rate
- Shorter- or longer-lease terms
- "Escape" clauses to allow you to get out of the lease in certain circumstances
- Free rent (one to six months, depending on market conditions)
- Lower prepaid rent and security deposit

I suggest including several or all of these in your proposal. You're unlikely to succeed with them all, but it will establish a good position from which to negotiate and help you evaluate the willingness of the lessors to engage in meaningful negotiations. Make sure the lessors are aware that you are negotiating with other centers. After you feel you have gotten all the concessions you can get, choose the one that's to your best advantage and finalize the terms.

A word of caution in negotiating: It is possible to be too demanding and distrustful and thus sour a relationship that you will have to live with for a long time.

There is still a place for trust in business dealings. I have discovered that most issues can be worked out when both parties approach them with consideration for the other party.

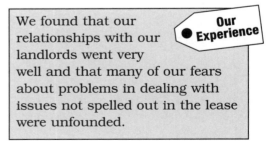

We found that our relationships with our landlords went very well and that many of our fears about problems in dealing with issues not spelled out in the lease were unfounded.

Our Experience

In negotiating a lease, it is best to deal with a reliable lessor. If a lessor has been in business for several years with a number of satisfied lessors, you can generally assume he or she will treat you fairly. Ask several present or former tenants about their relationship with your prospective lessor.

In summary, check out your lessor as best you can, try to define the terms clearly, have your lawyer review the lease, and then proceed with an attitude of trust.

Part 3: Starting Up!

Chapter 10

Money, Money, Money!

I f you are to be successful in the retail business, you must understand that everything does not happen linearly or in a distinct sequence. You must learn to plan, research issues, estimate costs, readjust, then go back, re-plan, re-estimate costs, and proceed only after you have worked out the issues to your satisfaction.

While it is logical to do your detailed financial planning at this point, after you have made decisions about location and leases and therefore have a pretty good idea of costs, it is also critical to consider your financial requirements and capabilities before you begin any detailed planning. In order to do this, you will need to use this chapter to do your preliminary estimate before beginning your search for a location, and then come back and refine it after nailing down more of the costs.

How Much Do You Need?

Your costs can be grouped loosely into two categories: one-time or startup costs and recurring costs. To help you estimate your costs, blank worksheets for one-time and recurring costs are included at the end of this chapter. Also included are sample

Our Experience ● Many of the costs shown in the samples are approximate actual values for our gift shops, which were located in strip shopping centers and featured a large number of items, mostly in the $5–$75 price range. Remember that these costs can vary widely depending on the particular line of merchandise and store location, but the illustrated amounts should give you an idea of what your own costs will likely be.

completed worksheets showing an actual range of costs that can be expected for a typical business.

Below is a list of items we suggest you include in your estimate, along with a range of costs you can expect, based on our experience. They will obviously vary depending on your specific business and location. The costs are divided into two categories: one-time and monthly. Before proceeding with your plans, be sure to take some time to fill in the blanks for both worksheets, remembering that they will provide rough estimates, not exact amounts.

One-Time Costs

One-time costs (startup costs) represent the amount of money you will need just to open the doors of your store. Table 10-1 is a sample worksheet showing one-time costs for a gift store starting in a low-end retail shopping center in a city of about 500,000 people.

The finish-out costs are material costs only for painting, some wallpaper, wood trim, and some special built-in features, with the labor supplied by the business owner. If contractors are used, this amount should be doubled. The sign estimate is for a lighted, backlit, block-letter sign with 15 letters about 14 inches high. Lessors generally have strict specifications for signs, with the lessee required to purchase from a supplier on a list of approved vendors. Pre-opening advertising includes six 10-second radio spots during morning or evening drive time, one 60-second radio spot, and eight 30-second TV spots during non-prime time hours. Initial inventory was estimated at about $13 per square foot of space. Display costs can vary widely, depending on the merchandise to be displayed.

Cost Item	Estimated Cost
Prepaid rent—two months (1,500 square feet at $.90 per sq. ft. per month)	$2,700
Security deposit (one additional month's rent)	1,350
Triple-net charge (12% of two months' rent)	324
Utility deposits (estimated two months' utilities)	300
Finish-out cost	3,000
Sign	3,000
Pre-opening advertising	2,000
Initial inventory	20,000
Licenses and permits	500
Display fixtures	6,000
Operating capital (about four months expenses)	20,000
Subtotal	$59,174
Contingencies (15% of subtotal)	8,876
Total	**$68,050**

Table 10-1. One-Time Costs Worksheet—Sample

If your product line includes furniture items, these can be used as display pieces, to minimize the use of fixtures. If you require special display fixtures, such as locking or refrigerated cases, your costs will increase accordingly.

Approximately four months' operating expenses were also included in startup costs because it will take a while for your sales to build to the point that you can pay expenses. The amount was calculated using the worksheet described in the next section. After

> **Our Experience**
>
> When we started our first store, we bought most of our fixtures at garage sales and flea markets and did most of the carpentry, painting, and wallpapering ourselves. If you have the time and skills to do this, you can keep your costs in the lower end of the ranges cited in the instructions for the worksheets. We also did not hire any employees at first, but added part-time help later on, after our cash flow was established.

adding all these estimated costs, a 15 percent contingency was added in order to cover unexpected or underestimated costs. It is better to have too much than too little at this critical time in your business.

Recurring Expenses

Table 10-2 shows sample operating expenses for the gift store described on the previous page.

Expense Item	Estimated Monthly Cost
Rent	$1,350
Utilities	160
Triple-net charges	162
Employee wages and salaries	1,360
Payroll taxes (7.65% of wages)	104
Sales taxes (6% of estimated sales)	660
Advertising	600
Bank charges	250
Insurance	60
Equipment leases	60
Miscellaneous	300
Total monthly expense	**$5,066**

Table 10-2. Recurring Expenses Worksheet—Sample

As mentioned above, rent is for a 1,500-square-foot store at $.90 per square foot.

Two part-time employees are included, working a total of 160 hours at $8.50 per hour. Payroll taxes are currently 7.65 percent of wages. This is the amount that you, as employer, must pay. You must withhold an equal amount from employees and transmit it, along with your share, to the IRS, on a monthly or quarterly schedule. The withheld amount is included in the total employee wages amount. There are also federal and state unemployment taxes. They usually are minimal and are paid quarterly, so they are not listed as specific items, but are included in miscellaneous expenses. Sales taxes are based on estimated average monthly sales of $11,000. In actuality, sales tax is not an expense, but is a pass-through amount that must be collected from customers and remitted to the state. However, since you will likely be including the sales tax as part of your gross receipts, it is included as an expense item for the sake of convenience and to ensure that you are aware of the need to remit it to your state revenue agency. Be assured they will not forget!

The monthly advertising expense is estimated at about 5 percent to 6 percent of gross sales for the first few months of operation. After startup, an amount between 3 percent and 6 percent of sales is probably adequate for advertising. Budgeting for advertising is discussed in more detail in a later chapter.

The item for bank charges covers costs for maintaining your checking account and the discount charges for processing your credit card sales. While they vary from bank to bank, they will normally be about 3 percent of credit card sales. Depending on your product line, credit card purchases will usually constitute 40 percent to 70 percent of your total sales. The expense item for equipment leases covers the cost for leasing a credit card terminal.

Other expenses—such as travel, repairs, office supplies, and subscriptions—are grouped in the miscellaneous category.

Sales Estimates

You will note that some of the expense items—such as sales tax, advertising, and bank charges—are related to your sales. This requires that you also estimate your sales. Estimating sales for a new store can be very difficult and fraught with uncertainties. Usually sales will vary within a range of $75 to $200 per square foot per year or $6 to $17 per month. For most stores, this is not spread evenly over the year. A typical annual sales projection for the 1,500-square-foot gift store used in the above examples might look like the amounts shown in Table 10-3.

Month	Estimated Sales
January	$6,000
February	9,000
March	10,000
April	9,000
May	9,000
June	6,000
July	6,000
August	12,000
September	10,000
October	11,000
November	20,000
December	24,000
Total	**$132,000**
Average Monthly Sales	**$11,000**

Table 10-3. Sales Estimate—Sample

Depending on what month of the year you open, you can see that sales can vary a great deal. If possible, you should consider opening in the summer in order to take advantage of generally higher sales volumes and still give yourself time to build inventory and gain experience before entering the highest end-of-year sales months.

Once you have estimated the recurring expenses, you should make a cash flow projection for the first three to six months of operation, using the estimates you have established in Tables 10-2 and 10-3. Cash flow simply means the sum of your income and expenses over a period of time. Table 10-4 shows a cash flow projection for four months' operation of the gift store used in the previous examples, assuming the store opens in May.

Merchandise purchases to restock (line 3 in Table 10-4) represents the amount you will need to spend to replace the items sold during the month. Since wholesale prices usually are about half of the retail price, these amounts are estimated at 50 percent of sales. Cumulative cash flow is obtained by adding each month's cash flow to the previous month's cash flow.

	Income and Expenses	May	June	July	August
1	Estimated sales	$9,000	$6,000	$6,000	$12,000
2	Estimated monthly expenses	4,700	4,700	4,700	4,700
3	Merchandise purchases to restock (50% of line 1)	4,500	3,000	3,000	6,000
4	Monthly total cash available (line 1 less lines 2 and 3)	-$200	-$1,700	-$1,700	$1,300
5	Cumulative cash flow	-$200	-$1,900	-$3,600	-$2,300

Table 10-4. Cash flow Projection—Sample

In this sample analysis, the maximum negative cash flow is $3,600. In May, more money was spent than was received in sales, leaving a deficit of $200. In June, expenses again exceeded sales by $1,900. This means that your total deficit at the end of June is $1,900. By the end of July, the deficit has grown to $3,600, before the higher sales in August reverse the negative trend. This analysis shows that you will need to budget $3,600 as one-time costs in order to cover your negative cash flow during the first three months.

If you are confident of your sales and expense estimates, you can use this amount in your one-time cost estimate worksheet as the figure for "operating capital." A more conservative approach would be to use three to six months' operating expenses for the estimated operating capital requirement.

After completing all three worksheets, you should have an estimate of how much money you will need to start your retail store, as well as estimates of monthly operating expenses, sales, and overall cash flow.

You probably need more money than you thought, don't you? Consider this just another example of Murphy's Law—everything always costs more than you think it will. Murphy is especially active when you open a business!

Where Will It Come From?

Now that you have an educated guess as to the amount of money you will need, you must decide how you will get it. You can finance it from your savings if you have that much, through a personal loan, or with a business loan. If you choose to use your savings, you are using what is known as *internal* financing. In addition to your personal savings, another form of internal financing is using the cash flow generated by your business after you open. As can be seen by the sample cash flow projection, it will generally take several months before a new store will begin to generate positive cash flow. In reality, most small business must rely on internal financing.

The other financing option, *external* financing, involves bringing external parties into your financing scheme. External financing falls into two broad categories, *debt* financing and *equity* financing.

Debt financing is usually a loan from a bank or other financial institution. Without a track record, which you will not have as a new business, banks will be very reluctant to loan you money.

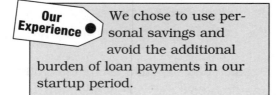

Our Experience ● We chose to use personal savings and avoid the additional burden of loan payments in our startup period.

Equity financing means involving an external party who will share in the profits from the business. Equity financing for a retail store is extremely difficult to obtain, unless you have friends or relatives who are willing to invest in your enterprise. It also involves allowing someone else a voice in running your business, a prospect that may not be appealing.

I strongly believe financing your startup without borrowing from others is the best course, if you can swing it. I have seen friends and associates struggle with those loan payments in the first year;

that extra burden can sometimes be the deciding factor in whether a business succeeds or fails. This is more a psychological argument than a financial one, because using your savings costs you in lost interest and can leave you short in an unexpected emergency. However, owing yourself gives you a higher comfort level than owing First National Bank—and you will be more lenient on yourself if you miss a payment!

If you need to borrow, you can explore the following options:

◆ Life insurance loans
◆ Personal loans
◆ Second mortgages
◆ Business loans

I have listed them in order of preference, because of cost and ease of acquiring. This may fly in the face of conventional financial advice, but again I'm not looking at it from a strict financial analysis viewpoint, but rather from a desire to avoid as many hassles as possible.

Establishing credit is a good idea, but without a strong relationship with a banker, a new business will have severe handicaps in obtaining startup financing from a bank. Without a track record, you'll probably have to put up considerable collateral to get a loan, so you're better off to use other methods, if possible, at least initially.

After you have an operating record, you should negotiate a line of credit with your bank and keep your banker informed about your business and its progress. That way, you can avoid having to go to an unfamiliar face in the bank to negotiate a loan if you need one to tide you over in a financial pinch.

This may seem like a short chapter on perhaps the most critical element of starting a business, but the brevity of treatment is not meant to underemphasize the importance of solid financing. If you do not start with enough capital, you will jeopardize the success of your business and any money you invest. Furthermore, the struggles you will experience in an undercapitalized business will not be pleasant.

There are good references in Appendix B on financing for your business. You should use them as needed.

You should also make several copies of the following worksheets and complete them in pencil so you can change and update as you refine your estimates.

Cost Item	Instructions	Estimate in Dollars
1. Prepaid rent	Enter amount from lease contract for prepaid rent or estimate the amount at two months of the average rental rate for your area ($.90 to $3 per square foot per month).	
2. Security deposit	Enter actual lease deposit amount or estimate at one month's rent.	
3. Triple-net charge	Enter 10% to 25% of one month's rent.	
4. Utility deposits	Check with local utilities for the amount of deposit they usually require from retail stores.	
5. Finish-out cost	Enter amounts not covered by lessor, such as paint, wallpaper, and floor coverings. Usual range is between $2 and $5 per square foot.	
6. Sign	Call a local sign company for prices. They can range between $250 for a modest sign and $5,000 for a large illuminated sign visible from a distance.	

Figure 10-1. One-Time Costs Worksheet

7. Pre-opening advertising	Costs can range from $500 to $2,000. Talk with a local advertising agency for different types of campaigns and costs.	
8. Initial inventory	This varies widely, depending on the products sold. The range is between $12 and $40 per square foot of selling space.	
9. Licenses and permits	Check with local authorities for costs and requirements for your area. The normal range is between $50 and $1,000.	
10. Display fixtures	Cost is highly dependent on type of merchandise and whether new or used. The range is $2 to $5 per square foot of selling space.	
11. Operating capital	Use results of cash flow projection or three to six months' estimated operating expenses	
12. Subtotal	Subtotal lines 1 through 11.	
13. Contingencies	Multiply line 12 by 0.15 (15%).	
Total	**Add lines 12 and 13. This is your total one-time cost estimate to open your store.**	

Figure 10-1. One-Time Costs Worksheet, cont.

Expense Item	Instructions	Estimated Monthly Cost in Dollars
1. Rent	Enter the amount from the lease contract for monthly rent or estimate the amount using the average rental rate for your area times total square feet rented. The usual range per square foot is $.90 to $3 per month.	
2. Utilities	Consult local utility companies for estimates. If you are renting a previously occupied space, the utility company can give you historical data for previous occupants. The lessor can also provide estimates.	
3. Triple-net charges	Enter 10% to 25% of one month's rent.	
4. Employee wages and salaries	Estimate the number of employee hours you will need and multiply by the prevailing wage rate in your area for retail workers.	
5. Payroll taxes	Multiply line 4 by 0.0765 (7.65% of wages).	
6. Sales taxes	Multiply average monthly sales (from Figure 10-3) by the sales tax rate in your area.	
7. Advertising	A possible range of advertising costs is 3% to 6% of average monthly sales estimate.	
8. Bank charges	Multiply your estimated monthly sales by 0.50 (50%) and then multiply that by 0.03 (3%). (This assumes that half your sales will be by credit card and that your bank will charge 3% for processing.)	
9. Insurance	Consult your insurance agent. Suggested range is $50 to $75.	
10. Equipment leases	This is primarily the lease on your credit card terminal. The range is $25 to $60.	
11. Miscellaneous	The suggested range is $300 to $500.	
Total	**Sum of lines 1 through 11. This represents your estimate of monthly expenses.**	

Figure 10-2. Recurring Costs Worksheet

Month	Estimated Sales
January	
February	
March	
April	
May	
June	
July	
August	
September	
October	
November	
December	
Total	
Average Monthly Sales (total divided by 12)	

Figure 10-3. Sales Estimate Worksheet

	Income and Expenses	Instructions	Month 1	Month 2	Month 3	Month 4
1	Estimated sales	Enter anticipated sales for each month.				
2	Estimated monthly expenses	Enter average monthly expenses calculated in Figure 10-2.				
3	Merchandise purchases to restock (cost to replace items sold during month)	Calculate as 0.50 (50%) of line 1.				
4	Monthly total cash available	Line 1 less lines 2 and 3.				
5	**Cumulative cash flow**	**Follow instructions below.**	*	**	***	****

*   Enter line 4 for month 1 here.
**   Add line 5 for month 1 to line 4 for month 2 and enter here.
***   Add line 5 for month 2 to line 4 for month 3 and enter here.
**** Add line 5 for month 3 to line 4 for month 4 and enter here.

Figure 10-4. Cash flow Projection Worksheet

Chapter 11

Legal and Regulatory Issues

Now that you have lined up your financing and leased your space, it's time to get down to the serious business of ensuring that when your doors open for business the first day, you have a name, licenses, and permits.

Business Organization Options

As a small retailer, there are three basic ways in which you can establish your business: as a sole proprietorship, a partnership, a LLC, or a corporation (either a subchapter S corporation or a full-blown corporation). Each of these forms carries its own set of advantages and disadvantages. Before you make a decision, you definitely need to consult an attorney, explain your personal circumstances, and ask for advice on the most appropriate business form for you. Here is a brief overview of each:

A *sole proprietorship* is the simplest and least complicated way to go. You do not have to take any legal steps to open a sole proprietorship. You simply open your doors and keep up with your income and expenses. At tax time, you will complete a schedule C to report your business income and expenses. You still must comply with all the tax and labor laws, however.

The major disadvantage relates to personal liability. Since your business is essentially an extension of yourself, you will be personally liable for debts your business incurs. The other forms of business organization limit your personal liability for business debts to some degree and/or spread the liability to other partners. There may be tax issues also, depending on your unique circumstances.

A *partnership* is the preferred form if you will have a partner in the business. It establishes legal obligations of all the partners and requires more legal documents.

A *limited liability corporation* offers a relatively simple means of incorporating to provide some protection for your assets, without thrusting you into the full-blown corporate mode. It can be done in most states using internet legal services companies such as Legalzoom.com. It does introduce additional reporting requirements. A review by an attorney is recommended.

Incorporation requires filing legal papers and establishes your business as a separate legal entity. The subchapter S rules for incorporation are much simpler than the rules for regular incorporation, but you definitely will need an attorney to draw up the papers and an accountant to advise you on tax matters. The primary advantage is the protection of your personal assets, should your business fail.

> **Our Experience**
>
> We chose to remain a sole proprietorship, mainly because of the inherent simplicity. We managed our debts aggressively and limited our exposure to claims and lawsuits through insurance and good management practices. Because I was working full time outside the business, there were some Social Security and self-employment tax advantages. And besides, we did not have significant assets that were at risk. We reviewed our situation with our accountant periodically and considered converting to a subchapter S corporation but never did.

Naming Your Business

"What's in a name?" Shakespeare asked. If he had been in the retail business, he might have answered, "Your destiny."

Perhaps that's overstating the case a bit, but a name can be an important asset in identifying and setting your business apart. A name deserves careful thought. It should, if possible, be descriptive, catchy, and easy to remember. You should be careful not to choose one that is too close to an existing business's name. Remember the old joke about the grocer, who, cautioned that he could not name his store Piggly Wiggly, chose Hoggly Woggly, instead? You may have also seen news stories about how jealously some national chains protect their names and trademarks, suing any and all who dare to copy.

Our Experience

We almost got a divorce over the name issue! Not really, but Susie did agonize, seemingly endlessly, over the choice of a name. Since we were starting a country gift shop, she wanted the word "country" in the name, for obvious reasons. However, there was another shop (not a gift shop) nearby, which had the "C" word in its name and she didn't want to appear to be copying. We were amazed by how many businesses that sell our type of merchandise, both wholesale and retail, use "country" in their names, thus limiting the possibilities for original names. So, off we were on a search for an original name that evoked instant identification with our merchandise motif. Susie must have tried and discarded a million names. (Sometimes I tend to exaggerate!) As we neared the point when we had to have a name, the increased pressure only made the name selection more difficult. Finally, she chose, in desperation, "Homespun Cottage." Both words evoke a country image.

This name served us fairly well, although several people have assumed we were a restaurant, a fabric store, or a needlework shop. By and large, however, it gives the right connotation and did achieve reasonable name recognition in our city.

Our Experience ● Susie was surprised at the process for registering our name in Austin, Texas. She went to the county clerk's office, was told to check several large ledgers to see if the name had been taken and, if not, to enter it in the book. And so it was done. We assumed there would be a computerized process for checking and cross-checking and that we would receive a gilded certificate bestowing our name. It's rather comforting to find that sometimes simplicity survives in the midst of a bureaucratic world!

While a name is important, it's not the be-all and end-all of your business. Try not to agonize too much about getting the perfect name. Conversely, it is important to think it through carefully and try to project how it will represent your business as it grows and evolves.

Once you get into the process, you will be amazed at how many businesses that sell similar merchandise, both wholesale and retail, use similar words in their name, thus limiting your choices for an original name that also says something about your business. It's a little like naming a new baby: most of the good ones have already been used. Unlike naming children, where you might want to avoid names being used by your close relatives and circle of friends, your business name has a much broader arena in which to operate. The possibilities for duplication are therefore much greater and more problematic. An internet search can provide information on duplications.

Our Experience ● We chose a local artist (a man with no apparent interest or understanding of our merchandise) to design our first logo, but it was rather blah and Susie was never satisfied with it. We later commissioned a female artist with an interest in our line of merchandise, who produced a very attractive one for a very small fee and we adopted it. It helps if your artist has some interest in your particular line of goods. Using a stock logo is cheaper and quicker, but we think it is worth the small amount of extra money to get a unique one.

Do the best you can on the name selection—but don't go into business as "The No-Name Store." Pick something and go with it!

After you decide on a name, you must register it, usually at your county courthouse or with your state Secretary of State's office. This is usually a simple process and will ensure that you don't duplicate another local store name. Procedures vary widely by political subdivision, so be sure to check with your own state or local jurisdiction or consult an attorney.

You will also need a logo for your store to ensure name recognition. You can either choose a stock logo from your packaging supplier, with your store name on it, or have one custom designed. This is another decision that can become troublesome, as you search for just the right image. If you are having trouble deciding, you can begin with a generic logo and perfect your own at a later date. There are a lot more pressing issues when starting a new retail business.

Registration and Licenses

If you plan to operate in a jurisdiction that levies a sales tax (as most do), you will need a sales tax number and perhaps a separate business license. The sales tax permit usually comes from your state department of finance, revenue, administration, or similar department. This is mandatory in order to be able to sell and collect sales tax, but it is also necessary to be able to purchase merchandise at wholesale and to get into trade shows. This will get you on the computer that sends out the forms for reporting and remitting sales taxes to the state government. In most jurisdictions, sales taxes must be remitted on a quarterly, monthly, or sometimes annual basis, depending on your sales volume. Your state may have different reporting requirements, but the agency that issues the permits will provide instructions. You may be sure that they will keep tabs on your business once you are on their radar screen.

You may also need business licenses and special permits from your local government. If a license is required, you may only be subject to a one-time fee and/or a small annual fee. However, some may levy a gross receipts tax and/or an inventory tax. The license is used as a means of identifying and tracking business activity and for collecting the taxes. Check with the planning or finance department of your city, state, and county for information on this. Don't try to ignore these requirements. The department will find you out eventually and cause you serious problems. Better to know about these requirements and plan for them than to ignore and have them come back to haunt you at a very inopportune time.

Insurance

Before you begin to accumulate inventory, you will need to have your business insurance in place. If you lease your space, your landlord will furnish insurance for the building and some of the common-use equipment and pass the costs along to you as part of the triple-net charges. If you own your building, you will be responsible for acquiring this insurance.

Your lease will almost certainly require you to obtain insurance covering losses to your inventory and the landlord's equipment that you are responsible for maintaining. Most importantly, the policy must protect you and the landlord from liability as a result of operating your business. Most leases will require you to include the landlord as a named insured and furnish proof of insurance to the landlord. Local insurance agents who deal in business insurance usually have standard policies that meet retailers' and landlords' needs and they are

> **Our Experience** ● When we experienced a break-in at one of our stores, the cost of replacing the plate glass was not covered. On another store, lightning struck our neon sign and the air conditioning unit, but neither was covered. These incidents led us to read the fine print in our policies and discover that the coverage is very limited. We really had no choice, however. The landlord required insurance and we needed the liability and catastrophic coverage. Adding all the smaller coverages would have run the price sky-high.

familiar with the notice and certificate of insurance requirements. Don't expect too much from a business insurance policy. Many of them have a lot of exclusions as well as hefty deductibles. Typically, policies do not cover glass breakage, although they cover fire damage. Some policies cover burglary losses, but not robbery.

The cost of business insurance, limited as it is, is not generally excessive. In a modern strip center located in a city with a good fire department, you can expect to pay a monthly premium of about ¼ of 1 percent of your inventory value. For example a retail store in the situation described above, with sales of $250,000 per year and an average inventory of $50,000 should pay around $125 per month or less. Check with local reputable agents for quotes.

In addition to general business licenses, there may be other registration and licensing requirements for certain types of businesses. For example, if you sell chemicals or pesticides or operate a dry cleaner, you will likely be subject to regulation by state or federal environmental agencies, in addition to the normal business licenses. Be sure to check with your local government and your attorney, if in doubt.

Now that you have successfully navigated the maze of legal and regulatory requirements, you can prepare to open your store.

Chapter 12

Purchasing Your Inventory

N ow that you have a name, several numbers, permits, and licenses, all you need is some "stuff" to sell.

Merchandise Markets

Unless you plan to market a very specialized product, the best place to gain access to most products is at "market." These are regional market centers with showrooms similar to retail shops, but here they sell only to bona fide retailers. Most showrooms represent many companies and individuals with products to sell. The major market centers—such as Dallas, Atlanta, Chicago, New York, and Los Angeles—are large complexes with goods ranging from jewelry to furniture. Small regional markets are also scattered throughout the country in larger cities. (See Appendix C for a representative list.) In addition to the permanent showrooms, most market centers have "shows" throughout the year, usually in January, July, and September, during which hundreds of "temporary" exhibitors display their work. Most major markets do not allow buyers to take merchandise back to their stores; you'll need to place orders for later shipment. In recent years, however, some have established "cash-and-carry" sections, from which buyers can carry merchandise home. This works well if you have driven a vehicle with sufficient hauling capacity to the market. Obviously, this will not work well if you fly to the city where the market center is located.

Our Experience ● I recall a couple of buying trips when Susie just couldn't resist buying stuff at the "cash-and-carry" section, and we ended up buying extra duffle bags in which to pack merchandise and check them on our flights home (over my protests, of course).

There are also wholesale markets that follow a "circuit" across the country, featuring products supplied by individual exhibitors. These are particularly numerous in the handmade merchandise fields. They typically appear in certain cities at the same times each year, often in the same venues.

Because markets sell only to retailers, you will be required to produce evidence that you are one. Usually, you must present a sales tax certificate, along with printed checks, letterhead, and/or business cards, in order to gain access as a buyer. You can do this on your first trip or in advance through the mail. You will be issued a market card, similar to a credit card, for identification. Major markets provide a wide range of services to buyers, including reservations services for hotels, airlines, restaurants, etc., many of which are at commercial discounts.

We recommend that your first trip to market not be during a show, which is always crowded, hectic, and overwhelming, even to experienced buyers. Between shows, the pace at showrooms is slower and sales personnel have more time to answer questions and generally give you helpful advice on your purchases. Most showrooms have sales representatives who will call on you after they learn of your store. These representatives generally are well acquainted with their merchandise and can advise you on bestsellers and items that are slow movers. You have to use your own judgment, but it's not a bad idea to listen to their advice because it is not to their advantage to sell you merchandise that will just gather dust on your shelves. The bottom line, though, is that it's your money and your decision.

When we started our business, we placed our first **Our Experience** orders for goods at the Dallas Market Center, one of the largest in the United States. We have found that market center employees are eager to make life easier for buyers, no matter how large or small the stores they represent. Likewise, the showroom personnel have always been friendly and helpful and willing to assist new buyers.

We looked forward to our market trips, since they allowed us to get away from the shop and our kids and spend some time together, although that time is usually pretty much filled with research and buying. We tried to go to different markets to get a broader view of available merchandise and to allow us to enjoy different areas of the country. Buying trips to Boston, Atlanta, Pennsylvania, Indiana, and Tennessee have not only yielded some merchandise exclusives, but also given us some enjoyable sightseeing opportunities.

Some retailers opt not to go to the market centers, after establishing ties to several sales representatives. It is cheaper and more convenient to buy your goods sitting in your own store, but it can be a mistake to isolate yourself from the rest of the industry and rely solely on salespeople. The market centers provide a look at what's happening in your field and help you to keep up with trends, allowing you to stay current with your merchandise and anticipate changing tastes. In my opinion, the travel costs are well spent and, as a side benefit, allow you to have a sort of busman's holiday, away from the daily selling routine. And, it's deductible (most of it, anyway).

Planning Your Buying

Buying at a major market center can be an overwhelming experience, unless you plan your activities carefully and purchase your goods in an organized fashion. In the remainder of this chapter, I'll describe the process for planning for and making a typical trip to a major market center. Hopefully, this will give you a better idea of the process and help you avoid some of the "first-time jitters."

You should begin planning for market trips well in advance. Obvious chores are securing travel tickets and hotel reservations several months in advance, especially if you are going during a show because accommodations usually fill quickly. Consider taking advantage of the market center's travel service and staying in hotels that are served by free shuttle services. This eliminates parking and traffic hassles and is recommended even if you drive to market, as many do. The additional cost of staying in a nearby hotel is usually more than offset by the savings in fuel, parking fees, and wear and tear on you!

Several weeks in advance of the show dates, begin establishing your budget for purchases. You should first estimate the retail value of your current inventory (zero for your first trip), estimate sales for the months between the upcoming market and the next one, subtract an allowance for goods purchased locally or through sales representatives, and, from these figures calculate the dollar value of goods you should purchase. Because you will not have a track record on your first trip, you will have to rely on projections. Table 12-1 shows the calculation of a sample five month buying budget for a new store of about 1,200 square feet carrying a varied line of products and opening around August 1.

After preparing an overall buying budget, you should allocate the amounts to each month of the upcoming selling season, based on anticipated sales for each month, as shown in Table 12-2. When you place orders, vendors will ask for a delivery date. By specifying the month when delivery is desired, you will be able to spread out the arrival of goods over the selling period. Otherwise, vendors

Total Buying Budget Worksheet	
1. Estimated sales for upcoming sales season	$80,000
2. Current inventory retail value	0
3. Subtotal (line 1 minus line 2)	80,000
4. Desired retail value of inventory at end of period	30,000
5. Retail value of required purchases (line 3 plus line 4)	110,000
6. Wholesale cost (50% of line 5)	55,000
7. Estimated local purchases and reorders	15,000
8. Budget for market buying (line 6 minus line 7)	$ 40,000

Table 12-1. Sample Market Buying Budget

will want to ship immediately and be able to collect their money as soon as possible. As you make each purchase, enter the items purchased in the left-hand column and the amount of the purchase in the appropriate column for the delivery date selected, until the amounts are roughly equal to the budget for that month. Obviously, certain seasonal items must be sold in a particular month, so plan your delivery date carefully.

This is not a foolproof system, as some vendors will not honor your requested delivery date and some goods may not be available when requested. Because of these factors, allocating the deliveries by month is about as close as you will be able to get. Table 12-2 shows a breakdown of the total buying budget by month.

A blank copy is included as Figure 12-1 at the end of this chapter. Use it each time you prepare for market, to provide a buying target. After the first buying trip, be sure to enter the retail value of your current inventory on line 2 of Table 12-1.

In order to avoid going to market without some idea of what you will buy, it is helpful to make lists of products that attract your interest, from magazines and other advertising, for several weeks before markets. Many showrooms and manufacturers send out literature on new products before each show and advertise in the trade magazines. After you have been in business for a while, you can use your computer to generate lists of the biggest sellers during the previous year. A workable inventory system that will facilitate this will be described in a later chapter.

You should try to arrive at the market site the afternoon before the first full buying day, register, collect maps and listings of the vendors and showrooms, and visit a few. Before starting your buying in earnest, however, try to gather information and get an overall impression of things. If you are a first-time buyer, you could profit by spending a whole day in this process before spending a dime.

Surviving the Market Environment

You will find that you will walk many miles at market and your feet and back will bear the brunt of fatigue, so it behooves you to plot as straight a course through the booths and showrooms as possible.

Vendors	Buying budget separated by delivery month				
	Month 1 $24,000	Month 2 $2,000	Month 3 $4,000	Month 4 $5,000	Month 5 $5,000
Boyd's Bears	6,000	1,000			1,000
Dayspring Products	2,000	1,000		1,000	
Alice's Candles	3,000		2,000		1,000
Sam's Dolls	4,000		1,000	2,000	
Horner's Cookies	2,000				1,000
Bill's Chocolates	3,000			1,000	1,000
Curtis Mugs	2,000		1,000		
Jim's Placemats	2,000			1,000	1,000
TOTALS	$24,000	$2,000	$4,000	$5,000	$5,000

Table 12-2. Sample Monthly Delivery Estimate

Perhaps the most important single piece of advice we can give you is *"Wear comfortable clothes and shoes to market!"* While it is not necessary to set style trends at market, dress professionally, albeit comfortably. If you dress like a beach bum, you'll probably be treated accordingly. A professional appearance will signal the vendors that you are a serious buyer and may strengthen your negotiating position, if such becomes necessary.

Many of the booths offer brochures and price lists that you can collect for those things that are of interest but you are not sure that you want to carry right now. I suggest you bring a roomy but light briefcase in which to carry them. Accept brochures only if you are truly interested in the wares or else you will be quickly overloaded with paper, as most vendors will try to get you to take their literature.

As you make purchases, store the invoice copies in a separate compartment in your briefcase and enter the total purchase on the budget sheet to keep a running total. A pocket calculator is a must!

Many vendors don't have time to total your order and it is easy to lose track of your costs, unless you total the invoices. You should also make sure the invoice identifies the item purchased. This may sound strange, but many vendors use a generic form and enter only codes, not descriptions. After buying several thousand dollars' worth, it is impossible to remember what each

> **Our Experience**
>
> In our first trips to market centers, we usually arrived early on the day before it started and spent the rest of that day getting oriented and placing a few orders. We then would return to our hotel relatively early and plan our activities for the next day. Using the product lists we had accumulated, we looked up manufacturers' locations in the market directory and planned a route that minimized walking.

invoice covered. Vendor codes will mean nothing to you. Always try to enter a short description of the merchandise either on the invoice or on the budget sheet.

You should consider visiting the temporary booths first, since these are small operators that sometimes tend to take on more orders than they can produce and it's better to get your orders in early. After you have covered your route, then review your purchases, both amounts and kinds. Then visit selected booths to fill in the gaps. A good estimate for time required at market is about three days. Count on leaving somewhat bleary-eyed and very tired.

Buying Strategies

Most showrooms represent a number of companies, most of which require minimum purchases. Generally, this minimum is a dollar amount, varying from $50 to several thousand for some product lines. Most minimums will be in the $100–$300 range. Some companies have a minimum quantity instead of the dollar amount or in addition to it.

While minimum buying is a conservative practice for new stores, it has its disadvantages, too. Under-ordering a popular seller can leave you unable to meet the demands and the demand may have waned by the time you reorder and receive a new supply. If you have a strong feeling about a new item, you should order a large enough quantity to last until you can reorder.

Most companies will require you to prepay your first order or accept it COD (cash on delivery). After one or two COD or prepaid shipments, most will extend credit, usually on a "net 30" basis. This means they will ship merchandise and you must pay the full amount within 30 days of the invoice date. Once you establish credit with several companies, you should prepare a credit reference sheet, make copies, and take them with you to market. Many companies will grant credit on your first order if you have several credit references from familiar companies. Others will always require COD on the first order. Still others will never extend credit, although this is the exception.

You will find that virtually all companies pass along the freight charges to you (typically 5 percent to 15 percent depending on weight, bulk, and distance). This is something important to consider when buying an item that weighs a lot. The wholesale price may sound great, but when you have to figure in the cost of shipping, it runs up the retail price considerably. Some companies will pay freight on prepaid orders. Others offer special discounts on promotions and "specials." It never hurts to ask for information on any special terms.

Our Experience ●   In our gift business, we felt more comfortable starting by ordering small amounts to see how the merchandise would sell. Sometimes we ordered only one of an item, but generally two or three is the least we would buy, since one item tends to get lost in the displays. If you're trying to make "a statement" by having a substantial display of a particular line of goods, you will have to gamble on a larger number.

We bought a lot of baskets on our first trip to market because they filled up shop space and were inexpensive. We survived our opening and our first few weeks of operation probably because of dumb luck rather than good planning. Hindsight has convinced us that, had we budgeted more money for our initial stock, we would have made a better impression on those first customers.

You should visit the markets and place your orders in plenty of time to receive them before your opening. You should place your orders at least two or three months in advance, or further if your opening is near the peak Christmas selling season, when orders are slower in arriving. If you will have the sales representative mark the order "NEW STORE OPENING," the manufacturer will generally try to make sure the merchandise arrives by a designated date.

Other Buying Options

In addition to the market centers, some goods can be purchased locally from individuals and companies. With many retail products, there are local craftspeople who make things that you may be able to sell in your shop. These locally made items add a great deal of interest in your product line. Instead of buying these items outright, you may wish to take most of them on consignment. This allows you to increase your stock without cost and you split the sales price with the consignors, accepting a smaller markup because you do not have your money tied up in the items. This is a bothersome process, however, and requires more recordkeeping and dealing with a lot of sellers. It also requires you to sometimes turn down items into which people have put a lot of themselves. This can be stressful, especially if the makers are friends or customers.

Although you're probably wise to stick to established markets for your initial inventory, once you are in stable operating mode don't overlook opportunities for adventure and unusual buying opportunities.

You will also be besieged by individuals or peddlers trying to sell you their wares directly, during your shop hours. While you can buy some good-quality merchandise this way, be careful about buying off trucks and out of the trunks of cars. There is some possibility that you are being offered stolen merchandise or very bad seconds, which you may not recognize until the peddler is long gone. In addition, dealing with every peddler (or recognized sales representative, for that matter) can interfere with serving your customers; you should not hesitate to tell the vendor you do not have

Our Experience

While I have the typical male characteristic of zooming down the highway, looking neither right nor left, in my determination to get where we're going as soon as possible (even when there's no real reason), Susie is constantly searching the roadside and signs for opportunities to stop, shop, or just generally explore. So, on our trips, we had this constant battle of wills about getting off the beaten path. However, when we agreed to have an "adventure," it often produced not only an enjoyable time, but also unique merchandise that we otherwise would not have found. (I still would never stop and ask directions, however. There are some portions of the guy code I just will not break!)

On a trip to Atlanta, we stopped at a rather uninteresting-looking craft supply shop, only to find some very well-made furniture displayed. On inquiry, we discovered that the furniture was made in a remote small town even further off the route. After our usual struggle and the usual result (Susie won!), off we went to the factory, purchased a vanload of the furniture (at a good price), and we were back on the road, without any serious time lost.

On a trip to the Midwest, we took a very interesting side trip to the Amish country of Eastern Pennsylvania. Not only did we experience the awe of spending time in yesterday, we also found a line of inexpensive pewter jewelry that proved to be a really good seller for us.

So, our advice is to take time to follow some adventurous trails, smell the roses, and check the shops! After all, you're getting into this business to have some fun, as well as make money, and you should take some opportunities to enjoy your independence and perhaps reap some financial benefits at the same time!

time to purchase goods during peak selling hours. Suggest that he or she make an appointment to return when you have help or on a slack day. They can be persistent, but reputable sellers will be happy to accommodate your needs and desires.

The first visit to your store will leave a lasting impression on your customers, so you should ensure that you have enough stock to prompt them to come back. From your own experiences, you probably know that a retail shop with skimpy offerings does not draw you back as easily as a well-stocked one. Hopefully, these suggestions for purchasing your inventory will ensure that your store will be attractive and full for your first day in business.

Online Buying

Many wholesalers and manufacturers maintain websites on which you may place orders. Some of these also sell retail, so be sure you access the wholesale website, not the one maintained for retail customers. These websites typically require you to pre-register, and submit documentation that you are a retailer, or that you have an existing account with the site operator. Some companies may require you to do this in person or by telephone, but others permit online submission. Once you are approved, either by pre-arrangement or online, you will likely be asked to establish a password, with which to obtain future access.

From this point on, ordering merchandise is very similar to retail ordering. The usual cautions regarding security apply, so be careful not to submit too much information, particularly personal bank account numbers, PINs, etc, that could facilitate identity theft. Most sites will have appropriate safeguards for your credit card purchases, but be sure to inquire about site security if you have doubts or questions. To keep these risks in perspective, remember that we routinely give our credit cards to waiters, clerks, and a myriad other service personnel, who are probably more likely to use your information inappropriately than a reputable online wholesaler.

Be careful when ordering new merchandise online. It is difficult to ascertain the quality of items that you cannot actually see and touch. After it arrives, you are stuck with it, or you must go through the hassle of returning it. If you are ordering from a current or past supplier, or if you are simply reordering the same merchandise, these concerns are minimal.

Everything considered, ordering online is a very useful tool for an established retailer, and provides a means for quickly replenishing your stock as well as for discovering new, attractive products.

Total Buying Budget Worksheet	
1. Estimated sales for upcoming sales season	
2. Current Inventory retail value	
3. Subtotal (line 1 minus line 2)	
4. Desired retail value of inventory at end of period	
5. Retail value of required purchases (line 3 plus line 4)	
6. Wholesale cost (50% of line 5)	
7. Estimated local purchases and reorders	
8. Budget for market buying (line 6 minus line 7)	

Vendors	Buying Budget Separated by Delivery Month			
	Month 1	Month 2	Month 3	Month 4
Totals				

Figure 12-1. Estimate for Market Buying Worksheets

Chapter 13

Preparing for Your Grand Opening

Finishing Touches

After ordering your initial inventory, it's time to turn your attention to finishing and decorating your store. Now you know, based on your inventory purchases, what kind of displays you will need. Most landlords will agree to finish out your space two to four weeks prior to the formal start date of your lease, to allow you to decorate and stock prior to opening. If you own your building, you will need to hire a contractor or arrange to do the work yourself. If you use contractors, you should keep up with their progress and make sure the work gets done on time.

You will also need to order your outdoor sign, do your special decorating, have carpet and tile installed, and move in your fixtures. Some of this work can be done concurrently with the lessor's work, if you coordinate with their contractors. Be sure to check with your lessor before you proceed, since many of them have very strict requirements as to what you are allowed to do.

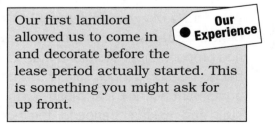

Our first landlord allowed us to come in and decorate before the lease period actually started. This is something you might ask for up front.

Our Experience

For example, most shopping centers have very specific specifications for outdoor signs and window displays, in order to control the appearance of their property. We'll discuss interior decorating further in the next chapter.

Other pre-opening chores include getting all utilities connected and transferred to your name, buying or leasing a cash register and/or calculators, and getting a credit card terminal installed and tested. You will also need to have your bank account established.

Staff Training

If your business will have any employees, you will need to recruit and train them for opening day.

> **Our Experience** ● We did not hire employees until well after our opening, preferring to handle the chores ourselves. We recommend this approach, if possible, so you can avoid having to get involved in payroll taxes right away and you can learn all aspects of your business before having to train employees.

If employees are a must for you, you should try to hire them in time to give them a good orientation to the job requirements and to your business philosophy. If at all possible, prepare an employee manual that completely sets forth your policies with respect to employee performance, hours, benefits, and customer relations.

Chapter 21 is devoted completely to employee relations and gives more details on how to deal with employees. In the pre-opening stage, the primary emphasis needs to be on training your employees and getting them ready for the first customers.

Even if you do not hire outside employees at this stage, you and your family members still need to have a common understanding of how to deal with all aspects of your operation. Try to anticipate and prepare for all situations that may arise. Have each staff member go through a mock sale to an imaginary customer, using all the equipment needed (calculator, cash register, credit card machine, etc.), and making change for the mock customer.

Advertising Your Opening

You should do as much advertising for your opening as you can afford because this will be a unique opportunity for you to introduce your store to your customers. It's a good idea to get your regular sign up as soon as possible so people can anticipate and watch the progress. Business and neighborhood sections of local newspapers may feature your shop, if they know about your opening. Call and ask about this possibility.

If your local laws permit, rent a portable sign announcing your opening and put it out three or four weeks in advance. Consider local TV media and newspaper ads, to run a day or

Our local paper ran a very nice article on our first shop, with photographs. This attracted a lot of interest in our neighborhood.

two before and after your opening day. If you can locate a small advertising agency, it would be a good idea to use them to help plan your advertising. A good agency will plan a campaign within your budget and help you get the most for your money. Their fees typically come from the media, not you, so it really does not cost any more. They also generally know about specials that you may not be aware of.

You may wish to serve refreshments or have small gifts during opening week; if so, include this in your advertising. Some other options for a grand opening, depending on the location of your store and available space are:

- Hire a local band to play
- Use costumed characters to invite people into your store
- Arrange for neighboring stores to hand out coupons, if they are willing to do so
- Have drawings for door prizes hourly

Well, are you completely ready for the Big Day? Probably not, but you'll survive it! The next chapter gives some tips on displaying your goods.

Part 4: Daily Operations

Chapter 14

Displaying Your Merchandise

Display Strategies

Appearance is so important in a retail shop that you should put a great deal of thought into planning and executing your displays. Master chefs are taught the importance of "presentation" of food. It's not enough that food be good and nourishing; it must also be appealing to the eye. That's why parsley growers survive. Not many people eat parsley, but tons of it is used as a garnish on platters of fish and other foods. Why? To provide a touch of color and make you want to order the dish.

Some restaurants feature color photographs of their specialties, displayed around their dining rooms. They are invariably colorful, balanced displays of their food that invite you to partake. Unfortunately, the real food doesn't always match the photos! But the point is that it's not enough to have useful, quality merchandise; you must display it in a way that says to customers "Take me home."

Imagination is the key ingredient to planning eye-catching and appealing displays. Don't be afraid to do something different, maybe even a little outlandish at times, within the bounds of good taste, of course. The more distinctive your store, the more your customers will remember it.

Our Experience ●

Susie was the unquestioned czar of displays in our stores. One craftsman tried to talk her into handling a line of doggie caskets in our gift shop. While that would have been distinctive and customers would have remembered it, she doubted they would have been motivated to return as a result of a pet casket display.

Even if you are part of a franchise, it's a good idea to add your own special touches to set your store apart from the cookie-cutter, stamped-out look of many franchises. For instance, card shops tend to look alike, so the ones that have used some imagination tend to really stand out in your memory. You may have noticed that some McDonald's restaurants have been decorated so as to add creative touches that set them apart. One that stands out as particularly attractive had a nostalgia theme, using antique toys, old pictures, and other memorabilia to achieve a very warm atmosphere in a normally cold and sterile fast food serving area.

Deciding on a Theme or "Look" for Your Store

Instead of mixing all sorts of displays in your store, you would be better served to establish an overall theme that unites your merchandise. All displays need not look exactly alike, but they should be compatible or blend in with each other.

This theme can go in many directions, from whimsical to very formal, with anything in between. It is determined mainly by the products you want to sell and the customers you are trying to attract. Have you ever been in a shop that really turned you off because the displays were random or uncoordinated, making you not want to come back? Naturally, you want yours to have the opposite effect and you want the look to be as distinctively yours as possible.

You don't have to settle for an unwelcoming interior decor just because the space you are leasing is plain, box-shaped, and finished in a generic and boring standard decor. Not many people are attracted to a shop that looks like a warehouse bay, unless perhaps you are selling industrial chemicals and forklifts. With a little imagination, you can transform "plain vanilla" into a "hot fudge sundae"! When you look at a rental space, train yourself to see beyond the obvious to the possibilities.

Lighting can be a key ingredient of any store's ambience. Most retail spaces are finished out

Our Experience

When opening our first country shop, we were not able to find an old house in a good location, so we had to achieve the atmosphere we wanted by using wallpaper, wood trim, and antiques to create a homey atmosphere in a plain "vanilla box" space in a strip center. Sectioning off the large space into small room-sized spaces gave it a warmer feel. We used furniture to achieve this effect. Lace curtains in the windows and rolling flower boxes set outside each morning gave it a cottage effect.

with commercial fluorescent lighting fixtures, which usually give a good level of light, but do little to add to a warm atmosphere.

Our Experience

In our stores, we reduced the number of fluorescent fixtures and replaced them with ceiling fans with schoolhouse light fixtures. We stocked a lot of lamps, so we used many of them for supplemental lighting in the room-sized spaces. This not only provided a warmer, more intimate setting, but also allowed us to display our lamps to best advantage.

We also built a unique checkout counter with a gazebo-like canopy that gave the effect of a cottage within the space. This was positioned near the front of the store, in the center, to serve as a focal point to customers entering the shop. In our second store, we used the same room-division technique, accented by false wooden beams between the dividers. We also salvaged some weathered boards from an old fence at our residence and applied them to the rear wall to achieve a lap-siding effect. We received many positive comments on the effects we have achieved using these rather simple and inexpensive decorating techniques.

All this is to say that you can make a silk purse out of a sow's ear if the desire is there. Consider this story about a woman who has a gift shop in a service station. The gas pumps are still bringing in a major portion of her income, but she has added a beautiful gift shop, carrying everything from small gift items to expensive collectibles. She enjoys seeing the faces of her customers when they walk in to pay for their gas—not your usual gas station!

A good way to get display ideas is to look around when visiting other retail shops. Go to other towns and look at shops similar to the kind you are planning. You may not want to copy their ideas exactly, but it may trigger a new idea for you. See what appeals to you and make a note of it. Likewise, note things you don't like so you won't make the same mistakes. Does this approach sound familiar? It should, as it's the way most people decorate their homes—looking around, filing away ideas, discarding things they don't like. Your shop may not be able to mirror your home decorating scheme, but it can reflect your tastes. This can be your chance to be a little bolder than you would at home.

You can get some pretty good ideas by going to trade shows and noticing the displays of the vendors. Some are really professional, while some obviously did not put much thought into displaying their wares. Trade magazines are also good research sources, or just magazines in general.

If decorating bores you or you simply can't come up with any good, imaginative ideas, you may want to get professional help on your displays. Some franchises offer this service and some may insist on certain forms of display, but even large card companies now give the owners some leeway to inject their own personalities into the atmosphere of their shops. Whether or not you get professional help may depend on your feeling of self-confidence in this area or it may depend more on your financial situation. If you can't afford outside help, brainstorm with your friends and family, develop some ideas, and go with them. Remember, you can always adjust the ideas later if they don't produce the results you want.

Permanent vs. Moveable Displays

After you have decided on a theme and done some research, it's time to think "permanent" or "moveable." You may not want any permanent displays; this is entirely up to you. This decision will probably depend on the type of merchandise you wish to sell. Moveable fixtures are more flexible and keep the store from becoming boring by looking the same all the time. This is important in gift, decorating, furniture, and other shops that depend upon creating an "ambience" to put customers in a buying mood and to illustrate ideas for using their products. If you're selling hardware, paint, or garden tools, this is obviously not a critical consideration, so permanent display racks may work just fine.

If you sell products for indoor use, you can use furniture for a good portion of your displays. The furniture can even be for sale, but sometimes, when a display piece is so covered up with merchandise, the customer may not realize it is for sale. So if you choose this method, make sure the for sale sign on the display piece is obvious.

It is probably a good idea to have a mixture of permanent and moveable displays. This combination approach will provide you with some needed flexibility, while minimizing the work of constantly putting displays up and tearing them down.

If you need display pieces that you are not able to build, look in your phone book Yellow Pages under "Store Fixtures" for companies that specialize in

Our Experience

At times we found we were not super successful in selling our furniture, a limited number of pine reproduction pieces. We suspected it was because our shop was so full of smaller merchandise that it was hard for potential buyers to focus on the furniture. We experimented with setting up a separate furniture-only area, with only enough accessories around to accentuate the furniture. This strategy seemed to be fairly successful, but it was hard to tell if the increased furniture sales compensated for the loss of the display space for our gift items and accessories.

fixtures of all kinds, both new and used. You may also be able to find local cabinetmakers or craftspeople to custom-build the items that you need. Other useful sources are garage sales, flea markets, and auctions. One advantage of a country shop or one selling retro merchandise is being able to pick up old, primitive items that can be used to enhance your look, often at bargain prices. In these times of nostalgia, older pieces can still provide attractive displays, even if your products don't exactly fit a retro theme.

Our Experience ● Among our favorite finds were some old kitchen cabinets that were in terrible shape, with peeling paint, nail holes, etc. We scraped most of the old paint off and repainted them. We used them to display our gourmet and country food lines and they were a source of many compliments from customers. We finished the country kitchen look by building primitive base cabinets with old feed sack curtains instead of doors, fitted with an old sink and water faucet. The whole display cost less than $50, proving that you can be creative and frugal at the same time. We knew we had achieved the homey look we were seeking when customers told us they would like to live in our shop.

Keeping Displays Fresh

You should be constantly researching new ways to display. Whenever you travel to a new town, take in the local shops to pick up new ideas. You can't let your displays become stagnant. You must be constantly updating and changing them to keep customers interested.

Old merchandise moved to a new spot will sometimes make the customers think it is newly arrived and pay more attention to it. This sounds strange, but it really works. This is an especially effective strategy for regular customers who come in frequently. Maintaining regular customers is another reason to keep a steady stream of new merchandise coming into your store. Many of them will come in and simply ask, "What new things have arrived since my last visit?"

Store Layout Strategies

Now you're ready to decide on a floor plan. The most efficient method is using a graph of the floor dimensions, drawn on graph paper. Measure your display pieces, sketch them on paper to the same scale as the floor plan, and cut them out. Then place them on the graph and move them around to find the most effective placement. Moving displays on paper is a whole lot easier on the back and the nerves than physically moving them.

Keep in mind that you need a smooth-flowing traffic pattern. This should determine where to place the displays and the checkout counter. In most instances, it is more attractive to have something set up in the center section along with things against the walls. It is pretty boring to walk into a shop where everything is displayed against the outer walls. Plus, you lose a lot of good display area. Be careful not to put breakable items on an unsteady surface where people can bump into them; that is a commonsense rule of display.

When possible, try to match products with displays. For instance, you could display foods, magnets, spice trivets, and cookbooks in an area of your store decorated with a kitchen theme. You can set up similar areas for children's clothes and toys, adult clothing, and jewelry, each decorated with a compatible theme. Highly pilferable items should be located where you can see and control access to them, such as at your checkout counter.

Your checkout counter should be located toward the front of your store, so that you can greet customers individually as they come in the door. Even in a commercial situation, people have a need to be recognized and acknowledged. Be careful not to appear pushy or put pressure on them to buy, but do acknowledge their presence, let them know you are glad they came and that you are there to help or answer questions if they need you.

Window Displays

Window displays are very important. Make them interesting enough to encourage people to come in and see what else you have for them. However, it is also important that potential customers not be able to see everything in the store from the front window or else they may be reluctant to come inside. Window displays should pique customers' interest and make them want to explore a little further by coming inside. One expensive mistake you can avoid is putting something in your window that is susceptible to fading or sun damage, if your store frontage is exposed to direct sunlight.

Our Experience The lace curtains we had in our first shop were an amazing drawing card that brought into the shop customers who were just passing by in their cars. We sold the lace in our shop, so we received double the benefits, attracting people to our shop with a product that is also for sale. If curtains are appropriate to your shop, take time to plan them so they will attract attention from several yards away.

Our Experience Our Christmas decorations went up in November, in conjunction with our annual Christmas Open House. After closing, on the night before our Open House, we worked like little elves—well, maybe not so little—to put up the tree, get out the greenery and all the Christmas merchandise, and generally trim the shop in the holiday spirit. This was a pretty tiring venture, but well worth the effort.

Seasonal Displays

Seasonal displays can be great fun and a lot of work. Choose the special holidays that will work best for you and concentrate on them. For most retail stores, Christmas sales are the highest of the entire year, so you will want to put the most time and effort into your Christmas decorations.

If you have a special Christmas event, you need to have a date in mind when ordering your Christmas merchandise. This is usually done in July—which is pretty hard to get used to—and you will need to specify a shipping date to ensure arrival in plenty of time.

Not all holidays are good for all businesses, so you will need to determine which ones hold the most potential for sales and concentrate on them. Flower shops typically have huge sales around Mother's Day and Valentine's Day. Hardware stores don't; they tend to do better around Father's Day, the fourth most important gift holiday,

> **Our Experience**
>
> We found our best times seemed to be Christmas, Valentine's Day, Mother's Day, and the end of school, when we sold a lot of teachers' gifts. We concentrated on these holidays and emphasized others to a lesser degree.

after Christmas, Mother's Day, and Valentine's Day.

Your seasonal displays can be little more than a table decorated with gifts suitable for that special time or occasion. Set in a highly visible space, this may be sufficient for your store, if you are not heavily into seasonal merchandise.

Display Talents

Displays call for creative talents that not all of us possess. If your talents do not lie in this area, it is important to recognize it. If you have others involved in your business, such as a spouse or another family member who does have creative talent, consider dividing the work accordingly. This will greatly improve display quality, not to mention preserving tranquility in family relationships. If no one in your business is creatively inclined, you should enlist someone with a flair for decorating to assist you in planning and setting up your displays. Some knowledge can be acquired in these areas through study and seminars, but excellence in display skills comes more from innate ability than learning.

Pricing Your Products

Pricing Policies and Procedures

You often see or hear retailers' advertisements that promise you "quality merchandise at a fair price." Well, just what is a "fair price?" As you enter the retailing arena, you will soon learn that there really is no universally accepted definition. Most of the time the answer is "It depends . . ." It depends on how much you paid for the merchandise, who you bought it from, what your competitors are charging, your overhead expenses, your sales volume, and a hundred other variables.

How you establish prices for your merchandise will be one of the most important decisions you will make, since it directly affects that all-important variable, profit. You must strike a delicate balance, setting a price that is high enough to allow you to achieve a reasonable profit margin and yet low enough to keep your merchandise affordable and competitive.

Even though there is no hard and fast rule for pricing merchandise, most retailers use a 50 percent markup, known in the trade as keystone. What this means, in plain language, is doubling your cost to establish the retail price. Because markup is figured as a percentage of the sales price, doubling the cost means a 50 percent markup. For example, if your cost on an item is $1, your selling price will be $2. 50 percent of $2 is $1, which is your markup.

This definition of markup was probably developed to avoid using a term that admits to a 100 percent increase. Most consumers would be appalled that you are selling something for double what you paid for it. They would be inclined to ask why you don't carry a gun and wear a mask. Most consumers have had no exposure to the myriad costs associated with retailing and they are used to thinking in terms of net profit margins they have heard in the media. For example, an article in the business section of a newspaper might report that Mega-Mart had sales of $500 million and earned a net profit of 4 percent. An uninitiated reader might conclude that Mega-Mart marks up its goods only 4 percent. In reality, net profit is calculated after overhead expenses have been subtracted from gross profit (total sales less cost of merchandise). Chapter 19 will explain in detail how to compute all these numbers and prepare a profit and loss statement for your business. Definitions of gross and net profit are included in the glossary for ready reference.

> **Our Experience** ● One of our customers offered to sell us hand-made items for $10 and suggested we could sell them for $12 and make a tidy $2 profit! We didn't bother to tell this person that we would be losing money after subtracting our expenses.

Because of these common misconceptions about pricing on the part of the buying public, don't be surprised that some of your customers think you are Jack the Ripper when they find out about your markup.

Although it is true that higher volumes will make up for lower prices to some extent, unless you can sell as much as a Kmart or Walmart, you absolutely need at least a 50 percent markup (keystone) to survive in a small retail shop. Although doubling the price may sound outrageous, it does not result in excessive profits when you consider the expenses for rent, taxes, insurance, supplies, labor, etc., that you must pay.

Sometimes you will have to sell an item at a lower markup, if you believe you cannot compete at a full keystone markup. Be careful, however, not to price too many items this way or you'll find nothing left for yourself at the end of the year. You can try to balance it out by mark-ing some items up slightly higher to compensate for

Our net profit margins usually ranged from 9 percent to 15 percent, using a 50 percent marku~ ~~en though we targeted a 50 percent gross profit (gross sales less the cost of goods), the actual figure ran about 47 percent, because of unrecovered freight costs and the fact that you cannot mark up every item 50 percent because of competition and your market's ability to pay.

the lower markups on others. You can do this when you get a spe-cial discount or are able to buy items direct from a manufacturer.

If you decide to use a markup other than the standard keystone (50 percent), here is a quick way to calculate your selling price:

selling price = [(cost of item) ÷ (100 – markup percentage)]
× 100

For example, assume an item costs you $10 and you want to use a markup of 35 percent. The selling price would then be calcu-lated as follows:

selling price = [(10.00) ÷ (100 - 35)] × 100
selling price = (10.00 ÷ 65) × 100 = $15.38

Do not multiply the cost by 35 percent and add that amount to the cost. That will produce a retail markup of 17.5 percent, not the desired 35 percent.

Don't overlook freight costs in your cost of merchandise. If your competition will allow, add the freight cost before you apply the markup. Most of the time, however, you will simply have to add freight to the marked-up price, thus recovering only the cost of the freight.

Exceptions to Standard Pricing

One area where pricing policy must remain flexible and where you can frequently achieve much greater markups is in collectibles and limited editions. If you have a hot collectible item, its market value will increase markedly as it goes out of production or print and you will be able to take advantage of the increased demand in your pricing policies.

Examples of items that frequently increase in value are limited edition prints, dolls, figurines, and antiques of all kinds. A word of caution here: Resist the temptation to exact outrageous prices just because you have a scarcity. This may gain some short-term profits at the expense of long-term customer patronage. The demand for items can also change suddenly, or over a short period of time. An example that comes to mind is the "Beanie Babies" craze that swept the country a few years back. It was almost impossible to buy them when they came on the market, and then only at outrageous prices. Now, collections of "Beanie Babies" can be bought well below original retail.

> **Our Experience** ● We rarely increased a price because it was in short supply and then only modestly, to help compensate for reduced markups on other items. We also opted not to invest heavily in "Beanie Babies."

Your customers will appreciate the fact that you keep your prices fair, when other stores are jacking up prices on hard-to-get items. This strategy will pay off in customer loyalty and increased sales, as they develop trust in the fairness of your pricing policies.

Consignment, as mentioned in Chapter 12, is the practice of allowing sellers to place merchandise in your store, for sale, with payment to be made only after you sell it. It may be to your advantage to take a limited amount of such items if your customers like the idea of buying locally made crafts. Because you do not pay for it until it sells and you have nothing at risk, you can set a lower markup, if you choose to do so. A common markup for consignment items is 35 percent. Remember: this means that you will take 35 percent of the retail sale price as your portion. Use the formula given above to compute the retail sale price.

You need to set up careful records to keep track of these sales and have an agreement with the consignors as to when payments will be made, who is responsible for loss or damage, and how long an item is allowed to stay without selling. It is recommended that you have each consignor sign a written agreement acknowledging the terms, before accepting the merchandise. This can eliminate misunderstandings later.

If you accept consignment items, don't allow them to push your own merchandise off the shelves!

One advantage to consignment is that consignors are also customers: They will be coming in frequently to check on their merchandise and are likely to make purchases during these visits.

This can also be a disadvantage, since some consignors, in their understandable zeal to have their products sell, may want to control the display and placement of their goods in your store. It is important to retain control over your displays; written agreements with consignors can reduce friction in this area.

> **Our Experience**
>
> We took only a few consignment items. We paid our consignors on the 10th of each month following the sale and generally assumed liability for losses. We had written agreements that required consignors to remove their items at our request. If an item had not sold in two to three months, we usually asked the consignor to pick it up.

Chapter 16

Customer Relations

There are a seemingly endless number of questions that arise and decisions that must be made when entering the retail business. Many of them relate to your relationships with your customers. Among them are:

- Credit or cash
- Layaways
- Damage policy
- Children in the store
- Hours of operation
- Accepting plastic

In addition to these basic nuts-and-bolts types of issues, you will also need to reflect on the moral standards of conduct for your business, otherwise known as business ethics. The first part of this chapter deals with the items listed above, while the latter portion focuses on some of the gray areas and questionable practices of retailing that you will want to avoid.

Establish Policies Ahead of Time

Unless you have been in the retail business before, you are likely to have no idea just how many decisions you will have to make about the day-to-day operation of your store.

> **Our Experience** ●
> Because we had no comprehensive guide when we started our business, we learned the hard way—by trial and error. We did not prepare a policy manual, so we had to wait for each situation to arise and then formulate a response. As a result, we made some mistakes and missed out on some opportunities.

You should definitely take some time before your opening to formulate your operating policies, put them in writing, and supply copies to all your employees. You may also wish to post some of them, such as policies on layaways and on accepting checks and credit cards, for your customers. Taking the time to anticipate and formulate responses to common, recurring situations will pay off in better customer relations and more profitable operations. Below are some insights and experiences in these areas, in the hope that they will be helpful to you in setting up some operating policies.

Credit

The summary advice on extending credit to customers is short and sweet: Don't do it! A new business owner has too many problems without having to deal with accounts receivable. Most people don't expect to receive credit in a small shop and will not be offended, particularly if you accept credit cards and offer layaways.

Layaway

Layaways are a good substitute for credit and without the risks. Decide in advance the dollar amounts and period of time you will allow for using layaways. You should buy layaway tags from your office supply store and use them to track these items.

Layaways require more storage space, especially just before Christmas and other holidays.

Special Orders

Special orders are another matter that you should consider, in setting up your rules for operation. They can represent a significant source of income, since customers are often willing to pay a premium price to pick out

> **Our Experience**
>
> We allowed layaways for sales totaling over $20 for 90 days, although we did not rigidly enforce these limits and tried to work with regular customers within reasonable limits. We set aside a special section in our storage room and placed layaway items on shelves, indexed by the tag numbers. We used a three-part tag, with one copy to the customer, one in a file box, and the other on the item in storage.

a specific color or style of goods that they need. If it is appropriate for your merchandise, it is probably in your best interest to try to accommodate most special orders. To do this, you should keep samples of items that can be obtained in different styles, colors, and sizes, where available.

There are pitfalls, however. Be sure to get a significant down payment for special orders (usually half the retail price), before you place the order. Otherwise, you may be stuck with unique merchandise when customers change their minds, move away, or simply disappear. Be careful also about special ordering a single piece, when you must order a large minimum quantity. If the product is a slow seller, you may wind up with a large quantity of duds in order to make a small sale.

Damage Recovery

You've probably seen signs in stores that say, "Lovely to look at, delightful to hold. If you break it, we mark it sold" or something

> **Our Experience**
>
> We carried lace curtains that were sold only by the half-bolt (about 15 yards). Therefore, we were reluctant to special order two or three yards, unless we were confident we would eventually sell the rest of the bolt.

equally cutesy. While this may give some shop owners some satisfaction, such attitudes and policies actually cost money through ill will and reduced patronage and sales and they are out of place in today's marketplace. Customers know that most merchants are willing to treat customers with respect and consideration and that they don't have to accept substandard treatment. Your best course is to simply grit your teeth, smile, and graciously accept your loss when a customer or his or her offspring breaks something in your store.

Speaking of damage, Rambo himself cannot inflict as much to your merchandise as a determined three- or four-year-old whose mother or father doesn't seem to notice or care that the child is bent on wasting your premises. While we still don't suggest you impose damages on the little tykes or their parents, do take steps to minimize the destruction. First, try providing child-size tables and chairs, along with coloring books, crayons, and children's books to keep the little darlings occupied. Suggest this activity as soon as parents enter the store. If a child is simply running wild, you might politely suggest that he or she might get hurt, hoping the parent will get the hint. If not, try to move stuff out of reach and pray that Mom remembers that roast in the oven and leaves. People are more easily offended over their children than almost anything else, so we counsel extreme caution in dealing with these situations.

Hours of Operation

You should set your hours of operation and post them conspicuously. The hours you decide to keep will vary depending on your location, the hours of neighboring stores, your community customs, and your lessor's rules. In order to determine your best hours to be open, keep track of sales versus time of day for several months and adjust your hours accordingly. If you are the only employee, give due consideration to human endurance. Don't try to push yourself beyond your limits or you will be faced with illness brought on by fatigue and it may cost you more to pay substitutes, if you can get them, than to reduce your work hours.

Credit and Debit Cards

You may as well resign yourself to accepting major credit cards! While it costs you to process them, the American consumer has come to rely on them, so you will miss out on too many sales if you don't take them.

In this day of advanced communication and technology, it makes sense to start out with the best technology available and avoid a lot of paperwork and lost time in registering credit card sales. Most banks can provide credit card services along with a terminal for your store. You can purchase a terminal outright or obtain it through a lease-purchase agree-

> **Our Experience**
>
> We accepted MasterCard, Visa, American Express, and Discover, although we added the last two only as more and more customers wanted to use them. We started out using a manual imprinter, which was adequate for the first couple of years. As sales increased and technology developed, we went to a terminal in each store that instantly read the card, issued the receipt, and credited our bank account.

ment. Most banks and credit card processing companies will furnish the terminals under a monthly payment plan. The discount rate—the processing fee charged by the credit card companies— is lower when you use the electronic terminals than when you process credit sales manually. They also are much faster and do not require telephone authorization for large purchases, as the manual charges do.

You should also arrange with your bank to accept all the major cards mentioned above. MasterCard and Visa are the easiest to obtain and use and are usually processed by the same financial service. American Express and Discover typically have different fiscal agents and will be reported separately, complicating your life somewhat.

Shop around for the best rate—typically 1.5 percent to 3 percent—and a bank or organization that takes all of the cards you wish to accept. Careful shopping for your credit card processor can yield significant dividends, since a fraction of a percent difference in the discount rate can save a lot of money over the long haul.

Some credit cards are most prevalent in particular locations; you will be wise to accommodate the prevailing plastic of your customers. For example, American Express has traditionally been the card of choice for business travelers and upper-income consumers, although that is changing somewhat with the increasing popularity of Visa and MasterCard, especially the Gold and Platinum versions. However, if you are in a resort or convention location or if you cater to high-income customers elsewhere, it would be wise to include American Express and Diners Club cards in your list of accepted cards.

Debit cards are essentially instant checks, in that the amount of the purchase is immediately deducted from the holder's account and credited to the merchant, either instantly or at a later date. Your credit card processor can usually handle debit card transactions, using the same procedure as for credit cards, although the terminal must usually accommodate entry of a PIN number for debit cards.

Other means of payment, using smartphone apps or other digital transfer devices may someday eliminate credit and debit cards altogether, but the small retailer may not wish to begin with such cutting edge technology, and the foreseeable future will undoubtedly require continued use of on-site terminals for those consumers who do not wish to give up their plastic.

Gift Wrapping

Whether or not to have a gift-wrapping service is another decision you may need to make. If you operate a gift shop, it's almost a necessity to provide some form of packaging for gifts. You will find that the costs of attractive wrapping paper, boxes, ribbons, and gift bags are significant and that wrapping requires a certain amount of skill to produce an attractive package. If you possess the skills, you will then need to decide whether or not to charge for the service.

While most customers are willing to pay, you may opt to provide it as a service rather than charging. If you decide not to charge for wrapping, try to minimize costs by using simpler packaging, such as inexpensive kraft bags on which you place an attractive sticker with your shop logo and name. Decoration can be as simple as colored tissue and ribbons or attractive ties.

Gift Registry

For some retail shops, such as those that stock china, crystal, or gifts, a gift registry is a must. However, recent trends have seen gift registries blossom at hardware and home supply stores.

You should consider offering a gift registry so that brides and others can select merchandise they like for purchase by friends and family. Many family members use this service to help their spouses, families, and friends with Christmas and other special occasion shopping. Your registry can be as simple as a loose-leaf notebook, with pages filed alphabetically for each registrant, listing their choices. When an item is purchased, mark it off in the book.

Business Ethics

One final topic that deserves some discussion is business ethics. While most people are moral individuals and want to do the right thing, you need to make some conscious decisions about your business practices in some gray areas. Few merchants would deliberately cheat customers, file false tax returns, or commit other offenses that can be classified as black or white. Gray areas, however, occur frequently, and it will be up to you to establish standards of conduct for your business that reflect your ethical principles.

A seemingly endless series of ethical and moral lapses have plagued the United States government over the past few years, as one official after another is caught in compromising positions. Recent newspaper articles and television stories have reported a growing resistance from consumers to what they perceive as unethical business practices. Many states have attorneys general who are very active in prosecuting those who engage in deceptive business practices. Therefore, it pays to establish policies that are fair and ethical and that ensure fair treatment of your most valuable asset, your customers.

Questionable Business Practices

What consumers perceive as unethical may not always be the case. As mentioned above, some customers will consider it unethical to mark up your merchandise more than a few percent, because they're unfamiliar with the costs you must recover. Most of them, however, when you explain the situation, will recognize and grant you the right to a fair return on your money and labor. You should never be ashamed of setting policies that ensure this. Even if you are inclined to make exorbitant profits, competition will generally prevent it. Obviously, the concept of "fair return" will vary from individual to individual and there is no generally accepted definition. However, most people will not consider a net profit in the 10 percent–20 percent range to be excessive, given the risks and the investment you have in a retail business. In the final analysis, however, you must decide for yourself what constitutes a fair profit.

There are some practices, however, that many will believe are questionable, from an ethical standpoint. A few of them are listed below.

Continuous "Sale" Prices

You may know of shops where all or most of the merchandise carries tags announcing that the item is "Usually (higher price)" but is "Now (lower price)." These tags never seem to change, so one has good reason to question the reality of the "sale" price. If you ask if you can order more at the reduced price, the clerks tell you yes, giving further credence to the suspicion that it's not on sale at all, but is being marked up artificially to mislead customers into believing that they are getting a bargain. You do not want to do this! When you mark something down, it should be from your original intended price and should represent a savings to the buyer. Customers will come to understand this and you will generally have no trouble selling an item at a reduced price. Oh, there will be a few "dogs" that you can't unload at any price—and you will wonder if you were sane or sober when you bought them! But that is the exception, not the rule.

You should limit your sales to only a few per year—three or four—and they should last for only a limited time—one to three weeks, normally. If your customers realize that you have continuous or frequent sales, it will be difficult to sell anything at regular price and you won't be around long or you'll have to resort to deceptive markups.

Advertising Very Low Prices for Items When You Have Only One or Two

Customers resent being sucked in on a ruse. You should consider not advertising prices, basing the appeal of your shop instead on unique and attractive merchandise and displays, as well as superior customer service. If you must depend on price as a major feature, be truthful and have ample supplies of sale items.

Sensational or Misleading Advertising

How many fake "telegrams" have you received from recreational resorts, promising that you have won a new car, a house in the country, or a fishing boat, only to find out, if you actually visit the place, that you've won a $50 inflatable raft? Most people won't believe wild claims and will be turned off by them.

The best policy to follow is one that gives you a fair return, gives the customer solid value for his or her dollar, and treats the customer as a rational adult. While there may be some who like being fooled, most just want to deal in good faith with a merchant they can trust—and you will be well served to cater to this larger group.

Other People's Ethics

On the other side of the ethics coin, you will find that there are unethical customers and vendors with whom you will have to deal. Although it is tempting to retaliate in kind, resist it!

There's a story about a businessman who purchased a newspaper from the newsstand owner in his building each day, always greeting the man with a cheerful "Good morning!" even though the greeting was never returned. When a friend asked why he per-sisted with his greetings when they were never reciprocated, the businessman replied that he never allowed someone else to control his actions or attitudes. Accordingly, never let unethical conduct of others cause you to sacrifice your principles.

Customer Relations in a Nutshell

There are a lot of rules under which you can operate your business, but you can't beat that old retailing axiom that the customer is always right. And, although it may require lots of restraint and self-control, your business will be better off if you observe it!

Always try to consider any problem from the customer's view-point and consider the long-term implications of your actions. Telling off that obnoxious customer might feel good at the moment, but how will it affect your business in the long term? When in doubt, always remember the Golden Rule and treat your customers as you would like to be treated. Besides, the vast majority of custom-ers are honest, considerate citizens who are just as anxious to get along as you are—and they make it all worthwhile!

By thinking about the policies and standards you will set for customer relations, putting them in writing, and communicating them clearly, you will be able to approach each day with confi-dence and inspire it in those who work with you and those whom you serve as customers.

Risk Management

W hen most people think of risk management, they think of insurance. While maintaining good insurance coverage is important, it is by no means the only component of risk management. Risk management encompasses the entire spectrum of actions and policies that are designed to mitigate your risks. Most risks cannot be totally eliminated, only lessened or minimized. Each aspect of an effective risk management strategy will be examined in this chapter.

Insurance

Since this is the subject most associated with risk management, it will be addressed first. There are several types of insurance you should consider maintaining.

Workers' Compensation Insurance

Most states will require you to maintain this to pay the expenses of employees who are injured on the job. Your premiums will depend on your experience with employee injuries. Accordingly, you should take care to provide a safe workplace. Take the time to survey your premises regularly to identify any potential hazards and eliminate them. Be sure to provide your employees with appropriate protective equipment, along with training in the safety aspects of their job. You should provide safety rules in writing, either standalone or as a part of your employee manual. If your products include hazardous materials or if you use any in your operation, you must maintain information on them in the form of material safety data sheets (MSDS). These are documents that describe the characteristics, handling requirements, and health effects of each substance. These are available from your insurance company or materials suppliers as well as from numerous online sources.

Unemployment Insurance

This is normally administered by the state. You will be assessed a premium based on either a standard rate for a new business or on your experience with actual claims. When an employee quits or is dismissed, he or she may file for unemployment compensation. If an employee is dismissed for good cause or quits voluntarily, the state is not required to pay unemployment compensation. However, many states are quite liberal with this benefit and will pay unemployment unless the employee has committed serious infractions, such as assaulting another employee or you. You will normally be notified when an employee files and given an opportunity to oppose compensation, if you believe it is undeserved. Be prepared for an uphill battle. You should consider opposing claims if you can document your reasons well, because your future insurance premiums are based directly on how much has been paid to your former employees.

Casualty and Property Insurance

This insurance covers losses due to fire, theft, or natural disaster. You will need to maintain it as a condition of most leases, as mentioned previously, and there are strict limitations on coverage in most policies. Be sure to read the fine print and add coverages if you believe you need them. This will cost you, however, and you may find that the costs are prohibitive or coverage is unavailable in your area or for your particular business. You will also have a deductible amount that you must pay before the insurance kicks in. If you cannot get a needed coverage or if you choose a high deductible, you will need to set aside a contingency amount to cover any losses. It's not necessary for this to be in the form of cash; just be aware of the potential need and know where the funds will come from.

Liability Insurance

This insurance covers claims from others as a result of the operation of your business. Business insurance policies usually contain liability coverage, with limits and deductibles as discussed above. Normally the standard limits are sufficient, but if you operate a particularly hazardous operation or if you have significant wealth that could be in jeopardy in case of a large judgment award, you may wish to secure additional coverage amounts.

Life and Disability Insurance

While most people don't like to think about it, it is good practice to consider what would happen to your business if you, your spouse or partner, or even a key employee died or became disabled. If such an event would cripple or severely limit your business, it is a good idea to purchase life insurance on that person, using business funds. These policies, called *key employee policies* or some similar name, will pay proceeds to your business in the event of the death or disability of the insured and hopefully help your business survive until a replacement is available.

Securing insurance is always a balance between the coverage and deductibles you desire and their cost. If getting the coverage and deductibles will run you short of cash to operate your business, then you may have to settle for less coverage and/or higher deductibles. Remember, nothing is risk-free, so don't panic if you are unable to insure against every possibility.

Employee Theft

This is an unpleasant but very real problem. You can minimize the probability by hiring only people you know well and by checking

references carefully. Unfortunately, neither of these steps will eliminate the possibility that one of your employees will victimize you
by stealing. The best way to minimize the possibility is to have no
employees or only a few. The next best way is to maintain some
standard controls to detect losses from your cash drawer and
inventory. Among the controls available are:

◆ Maintain rotating employee assignments so that different
  employees are teamed together or with you.
◆ Have procedures for balancing the cash register or drawer after
  each employee's shift.
◆ Take physical inventory at least annually, more often if practical.
◆ Check daily receipts against a list of items sold.
◆ Randomly monitor the inventory of particular items and com-
  pare with recorded sales over a period of time.

If you suspect an employee of stealing, randomly audit sales
by contacting customers to verify sale details. You can do this as a
routine survey of customer service.

Don't become so obsessed with catching a potential thief that
you treat your employees with suspicion and disrespect. They
deserve to be trusted and treated with respect and confidence
unless evidence indicates otherwise. The simple controls outlined
above will not catch all pilferage, but they will usually disclose discrepancies, if you use them consistently.

Shoplifting

Shoplifting, otherwise known in the trade as the *five-finger discount*, is rampant throughout most of the world. It is almost certain
that you will experience it in your store; it is not a question of if, but
of when and how much. Shoplifting has become something of a
status symbol in certain demographic groups and a way of life in
others. Some young people, along with some of their elders, don't
see shoplifting as a crime, with a victim—you, the retailer. It is an
impersonal crime and is not easy to detect until after the fact.

Your vulnerability to this crime will vary with the type of merchandise you carry in your store. Furniture stores and other large-

item retailers have little to fear. If you carry small, easily concealed items that are attractive to younger people and to others who are professional thieves, watch out! Particularly vulnerable are stores selling music CDs, electronic games, and other electronic devices.

What can and should you do about it? First, take steps to reduce the temptation to would-be shoplifters. These include the following:

- Put highly pilferable items close to the checkout counter.
- Maintain a good line-of-sight to sections of your store where desirable items are displayed.
- Use packaging that is hard to conceal.
- Make your presence known throughout the store. Don't hound your customers, but try to wander through the store periodically, greeting customers in a friendly manner.
- If your losses warrant them, install mirrors and/or closed-circuit TV cameras to monitor all portions of your store.
- Consider using electronic tags with a sensing device at the door, if you are unable to control thefts any other way.
- Pay particular attention to people whom you do not know, people carrying large bags, and—it pains me to say it—mothers with strollers or baby carriages.
- Post signs stating your policy to prosecute shoplifters.

A word of caution is in order. Do not confront someone whom you suspect of shoplifting, unless you are sure—and then only when other employees are around and you have ready access to security forces. Do not try to stop a shoplifter when you are alone in the store. Some shoplifters can be dangerous when cornered. Recovering a stolen item is not worth endangering your life.

Since our stores carried mostly decorative items for the home, many of which were fairly large, we did not attract a lot of shoplifting. We did experience several incidents, some of them involving repeat thefts by the same family group, who seemed intent on sprucing up their spaces at our expense. We never reached the point that we had to install surveillance equipment, but we tried to follow the passive measures mentioned above.

Store Security

You should keep your doors and windows locked at all times when you are closed. Keeping a few lights on all the time is also a good idea. Many malls and strip centers have roving security patrols, so find out how to contact them and report any suspicious activity to them. Unless you are located in a high-crime area, bars and extraordinary security measures are probably not justified.

Always lock your doors when you leave. That sounds obvious, but sometimes people forget. It is easy to get in a hurry, become distracted, and walk out without locking them. It's a good idea to have a regular routine to follow at day's end, possibly using a checklist or a reminder on the inside of your door.

As we stated at the beginning of this chapter, risks cannot be avoided, only minimized. Take prudent steps to minimize your risks, but don't fret over them. Serious losses and lawsuits are rare, so don't waste your creative energies worrying about the possibilities. Put them to better use running your store and making profits.

Our Experience ●
Someone broke into one of our stores during the night and took a few items, including some blank, signed checks. We don't recommend this practice! We kept a few on hand so that employees who were not on the bank's signature list could pay for COD merchandise. We were fortunate to be able to stop payment on them before the thief could cash any. Our biggest loss was in replacing the plate glass door the thief broke.

Our Experience ●
We left our doors unlocked several times during the years we were in business. Either we discovered it the next morning when we arrived to open or the security patrol called to tell us. We also made several trips back to the store to check doors when we could not remember locking them. With all our lapses, however, we never suffered a loss as a result—just a lot of inconvenience and uneasiness.

Chapter 18

Day-to-Day Cash Management

The Daily Grind

This is not a chapter on sophisticated techniques for maximizing your return on invested funds. By now, you should be aware that you are reading a book authored not by a financial expert, but by an ordinary person whose goal is to provide practical day-to-day advice on starting and operating a small retail business.

Accordingly, this chapter will deal with those mundane, often trivial details associated with the daily process of exchanging the stock in your store for currency, checks, and credit card slips. There are other, much better sources for advice on the weightier financial matters involved in business management; we will discuss some of them in a later chapter. Here, I want to provide some suggestions on specific procedures for handling those daily financial chores involving receiving and accounting for cash, checks, and credit card charges and that distasteful activity, paying bills.

Managing the Cash Drawer

In your retail store, you can expect to receive payment in cash, checks, credit or debit cards, and traveler's checks. This section describes the details for handling each of these four types of transactions.

Cash

Cash may be the least common form of payment in these days of plastic and electronics. Although you may wish to take in more cash, receiving payment in electronic form is actually easier to manage, although it may be at a small cost. Regardless, you must be prepared to accept cash and to make change from your cash drawer.

The first question you must answer is how much change and in what denominations do you need to keep in your drawer and how do you replenish it each day?

For example, if most of your items sell for less than $40, you might start out with $125 in your cash drawer. This amount should be broken down approximately as shown in Table 18-1.

Cash Drawer Setup	
Denomination	**Amount**
Ten-dollar bills	$20.00
Five-dollar bills	75.00
One-dollar bills	20.00
Quarters	5.00
Dimes	3.00
Nickels	1.50
Pennies	0.50
Total	**$125.00**

Table 18-1. Sample Cash Drawer Setup

Whether or not you accept personal checks and debit cards will affect the amount and the denominations of cash you keep in your drawer. If you accept them, you will likely find that 50 percent to 75 percent of your receipts are checks and debit cards, thus lessening the need for cash.

If you do not accept checks and debit cards or your price range varies from the example, you may need to adjust your cash drawer contents accordingly. If most of your merchandise sells for less than five or ten dollars, you can probably get by with a lower total amount, although you will need more coins and $1 bills. If you carry very expensive merchandise, it will almost be a necessity to accept checks, debit and credit cards, which will reduce your change requirements.

In our gift stores, most items sold for $5 to $100 and we used the cash drawer setup shown in Table 18-1 for over 15 years with few problems.

Our Experience

Considering all these variables, the setup shown in Table 18-1 will probably work for most stores, even those carrying higher-priced merchandise, since most people do not carry large amounts of cash and will pay for expensive items with checks or credit/debit cards.

You should replenish cash each time you make a bank deposit, although you need not restore the distribution among the various bill and coin denominations exactly. Simply monitor each denomination and replenish each when it gets too low. You should restore the same total each time, however, in order to properly balance your drawer each day.

Making change for customers is one area where many mistakes can occur. Train yourself and your employees how to correctly count change back to customers, even if you have a modern cash register that calculates the change for you. You may have been in a fast food restaurant when the automatic cash register was not working and observed the difficulty employees had trying to make change when the correct amount was not calculated for them. You do not want this to happen in your store.

For example, if the purchase comes to $3.70 and the customer pays with a $5 bill, you would select a nickel, a quarter, and a $1 bill from the drawer. Then, beginning with the smallest denomination, you would hand the money to the customer while counting up from $3.70, saying "$3.75" as you hand over the nickel, "$4.00" as you give the quarter, and "$1.00 makes five" as you lay the dollar bill down.

Experienced cashiers always leave the customer's payment out until the change is counted back, since customers often forget whether they paid with a $5, $10, or $20 bill. Having the bill to show them avoids confusion and saves you and your customer from any embarrassing scenes.

Checks

You will need to decide your policy on accepting checks. If your business deals mainly with a local clientele, you can probably implement a rather liberal check acceptance policy, only requiring that current addresses and phone numbers be printed on the checks. With the right types of customers—and some plain good luck—you will most likely experience few losses, in spite of the numerous horror stories you have heard about bounced checks.

> **Our Experience**
>
> When we started our business, we had heard so many horror stories of bouncing checks that we implemented our rather liberal check acceptance policy with some trepidation. However, we are still amazed that we experienced hardly any losses due to bad checks in more than 15 years of operation. Checks were returned, but we were able to collect virtually all of them ourselves, with occasional assistance from our bank.

If you will be selling mainly to tourists or to a group of customers with known credit problems or if your area of operations has a history of bad checks, you should consider signing up with one of the check verification and insuring agencies that operate all over the country. Your bank can refer you to some reliable companies. Here are other precautions you can take:

◆ Require an ID or driver's license number. This way you can check that the address on the check is current, which will allow you to contact the customer in the event of a problem.

◆ Call the bank to verify that funds are sufficient if the check is for a large amount and you don't know the customer.
◆ Make sure the check is signed and the amount is correct.
◆ Deposit checks promptly.

Credit and Debit Cards

Credit cards must be accepted in accordance with your bank or processor's rules. Electronic terminals, which are likely to be required by your processor, eliminate most verification requirements for credit and debit cards.

Traveler's Checks

Traveler's checks are simple. The only requirement is that the checks be signed in your presence. Treat them like any other check.

Reconciling Daily Receipts and Sales

The next questions involve reconciling your daily receipts and sales and preparing your bank deposits. In addition to the cash that you take in from sales, you must also account for any cash disbursements you make from the cash drawer. While you should make most purchases by check, it is almost impossible to avoid paying for some minor items from your cash if you do not keep a separate petty cash account. You should record each cash payment daily on cash disbursement slips and later enter it on the books, right along with any checks written, as we will discuss in the next chapter.

Reconciling your daily receipts is a very simple process that only takes a few minutes each day. You will generally need to reconcile the following on a daily basis:

◆ Cash received
◆ Checks received
◆ Credit and debit card purchases
◆ Minor cash disbursements

All these will need to be balanced against your sales for the day. If you have a point-of-sale system or a sophisticated cash register, you may be able to use it to summarize sales into the above listed categories at the end of each day. If you do not have such systems, you can still get the job done using two part sales books. The following instructions assume use of sales books. If you have a sales system that provides a daily summary in sufficient detail, use that.

Enter each sale on a ticket, listing your inventory code, price per item, extended sales amount, sales tax, and the total due. Give one copy to the customer and retain the other one for your records. You can customize these tickets by using a rubber stamp to place your store name and address on the customer copies during slack periods.

At the end of the day, begin your daily reconciliation by count-ing up your cash drawer. Next, simply total all sales from your sales tickets or your cash register daily report, checks received, credit and debit card totals, and any cash disbursements that came directly from your cash drawer. Then, you can use a simple recon-ciliation sheet to complete the process, such as the one shown in Figure 18-1 or one you make yourself.

The daily reconciliation will help you determine the amount of your bank deposit and whether the day's cash transactions have been handled accurately.

If you are out of balance and cannot find the error, you should fill out a cash disbursement slip in the amount of the shortage or complete a dummy sales slip for the amount of the overage. Then, run the totals again, before making your deposit, and check your permanent change amount.

Although it is not good accounting, if you are only a few cents off, you can make up the difference from your pocket or take it out of the drawer to balance. This is considered very sloppy book-keeping, but your time is worth more than using it to chase down 10 or 15 cents. You will seldom have significant variances, and these will usually be the result of silly mistakes, like giving both copies of the sales slip to the customer. It is important to balance daily, so that you can pinpoint the date of any variances. This is especially important when you have employees and when employees and owners work irregular, alternating schedules. Otherwise, there will be questions and suspicions about when the variance occurred and who is responsible.

Cash Management Systems

As you can see, the cash drawer and reconciliation are simple enough that you probably don't even need a cash register unless you are doing an extremely high volume of business. Consider not buying a cash register until you are convinced that the cost will be justified by improvements to your cash reconciliation and controls.

The only real advantage to a cash register is the security of a locking cash drawer. If you want to keep up with inventory on a daily basis, you will still have to use sales slips, unless you opt for a sophisticated point-of-sale (POS) computerized system that can handle a diverse inventory. These systems are becoming quite affordable, but will require training for you and your employees. The more inexpensive systems are generic and require you to conform your inventory numbering system to theirs. This may or may not work for you. There are a number of POS systems specifically designed for different businesses, such as restaurants, bars, and video stores. It would be worth your while to investigate them.

All of the POS systems will require some effort to start up and run efficiently. As a new business, you should consider whether the investment of scarce human and cash resources in such a system is a prudent move. If you decide to use a more manual cash management system, you can always switch later, when your business is listed on the New York Stock Exchange.

However, if you just can't think of having a business without the presence of a cash register, several models are available for less than $300 that will satisfy basic requirements. Once you have a cash register, you can also use the register tape to verify your manual totals or vice versa.

That's pretty much it for this painful little exercise of daily cash management. It's not all that complicated, but it is one of the most important facets of your business, since your discipline (or lack of it) will have a big impact on your ability to manage your business efficiently.

Instructions for Figure 18-1:

Column 1. Enter today's date. One line is used for each day you are open.

Column 2. Enter the sales total for the day.

Column 3. Enter the total amount of cash in the drawer.

Column 4. Enter the permanent change amount to be retained in the drawer, for example $125, as illustrated in Table 18-1.

Column 5. Subtract column 4 from column 3 and enter here. This is the cash you actually received during the day, after removing the permanent change amount.

Column 6. Add up and enter all cash items paid out of the drawer during the day, such as petty cash, minor purchases, owner draws, etc.

Column 7. Add columns 5 and 6 and enter here. This accounts for the cash received and the cash paid out.

Column 8. Enter the total amount of all checks received during the day.

Column 9. Enter the total amount of credit and debit card sales for the day.

Column 10. Add columns 7, 8, and 9, then subtract column 2. The total should be zero. A negative total indicates a shortage; a positive total indicates an overage. If the shortage or overage is significant, recount and run the totals again.

Column 11. Total deposit (sum of columns 5, 8, and 9). This amount should equal the amount filled in on your bank deposit slip. If credit and debit card receipts are deposited electronically, your deposit will consist of only columns 5 and 8.

1	2	3	4	5	6	7	8	9	10	11
Date	Sales totals	Cash in drawer	Permanent change amount	Cash less change (col. 3 – col. 4)	Cash paid out of drawer	Adjusted cash (sum of cols. 5 and 6)	Checks total	Credit/debit card total	Balance (total of cols. 7, 8, and 9 – col. 2)	Deposit total (total of cols. 5, 8, and 9)

Figure 18-1. Daily Reconciliation Worksheet

Chapter 19

Financial Management and Bookkeeping

Now that you have the basics of managing your cash receipts on a daily basis, let's step back from the trees and look at the forest. In other words, this chapter will focus on the broader aspects of managing your finances, including paying your bills, financial reports you should prepare, and the basics of bookkeeping.

Paying Your Suppliers

Your bank account will look so good. . . and then it's time to pay the bills. In order to maintain a good credit record, it is essential to pay your bills when due. Be assured that someone is watching your credit record even though you are unaware of it. Credit rating agencies constantly monitor everyone who makes financial transactions. So, take whatever steps are necessary to pay on time. This is usually 30 days after your invoice date.

Sometimes, it is even to your advantage to pay a bill ahead of time, when the manufacturer offers a discount for early payment. An early-pay discount is usually specified in a notation on your invoice, such as "2 percent in ten days." This means you may deduct 2 percent of the invoice if you pay within ten days. You have to decide whether the savings is worth paying in advance or if you would be better off to hold payment the full 30 days, thus being able to use the money for a more pressing need. Most of the time, your invoices from a single manufacturer will not be large enough to realize that great a savings. Also, only a few manufacturers offer the early payment discount.

Some manufacturers require payment within ten or 15 days, but these are pretty few and far between. So few, in fact, that you may overlook this fact on their invoices and be late making payment, assuming it is the usual 30-day limit.

Deciding when the 30 days starts has always been a bit of a mystery, but to be on the safe side, you should figure this from the date of shipment. If there is a big discrepancy between the date of shipment and the date of arrival, you may want to assume that the clock starts at arrival. If the supplier complains, you can always explain the situation. Some suppliers try to accelerate payment by backdating their invoices.

By having a net-30 basis on most of your shipments, you have time to sell some of the merchandise before you have to pay for it. This gives you float time and hopefully enables you to keep your cash flow moving smoothly. There are times when this can get pretty sticky; for instance, when you have been to market and everything you have ordered comes in at once.

Always try to space out shipments when you order, but "the best-laid plans of mice and men often go awry." Some orders will come before you expect them and others will come much later. Mass arrivals seem to happen when business is the slowest and you have the least amount of cash available, making net-30 accounts even more important.

A word of caution: Be sure to check each invoice against the shipment because manufacturers do make mistakes. Most manufacturers require that you notify them about any discrepancies within a certain period of time. This includes shortages or breakage in the shipment, as well as bookkeeping errors.

Paying the Government

In addition to taking care of your bills from your vendors, you also have responsibilities for making your payments to the government. You will be collecting sales taxes and withholding income, Social Security, and Medicare taxes from employees, if you have any. Since these payments are usually due monthly or quarterly, it is easy to think you have a healthy bank balance, when, in reality, it is not your money, but Uncle Sam's and the state's.

You will have myriad taxes to pay, so you need to have a reminder system to be sure they are paid when due. These taxes will include income, Social Security, Medicare, withholding, self-employment, unemployment, and sales taxes. You will need to keep track of which taxes must be paid to federal, state, and even local governments. Spend the time necessary to set up a system for ensuring they get paid on time. You should consider setting up a separate bank account to escrow these funds if you are likely to draw your bank balance down to the point where you are unable to pay your taxes when due.

> **Our Experience**
>
> In our case, we did not set up an escrow, opting to attempt to exercise discipline in maintaining sufficient balances to make the tax payments when they became due. It was not a major problem, but there were a few unpleasant surprises! You may wish to discuss with your accountant or legal advisor the pros and cons of putting your taxes in an escrow account.

Preventing Cash Crunches

During your first few months in business—and really forever—you should do cash flow projections, as outlined in Chapter 10, and update them monthly. These projections should show both weekly sales projections, as well as weekly anticipated expenses, including payments for rent, merchandise, and taxes, preferably plotted on a graph to show net cash flow, both negative and positive. This will allow you to manage your bank balance to ensure that at no time will you be unable to pay your bills.

In actuality, you will probably face times when you will need to put more cash into your business to maintain a positive cash balance. This condition occurs most often before a major seasonal selling period, when you must build your inventory in advance of the anticipated increased sales. In retail, the most vulnerable time is in September and October, when you must begin paying for merchandise that you have ordered for the Christmas selling season. By mid-November, sales are usually up enough to replenish the coffers, but it can be touch and go for a few weeks.

Other cash crunches can occur at income tax time or after you invest in new fixtures, equipment, or an expensive line of goods. It pays to anticipate and plan for these lean times by retaining adequate cash in the business when times are good. Learn to recognize when the large bank balance is really an illusion and you should leave it alone.

Taking Draws

Now that you have paid everyone else and you have planned for maintaining a positive cash balance, you are probably wondering when you will get paid. When you take money out of your business, it is known as a *draw*.

Don't yield to the temptation to take money out right away, just because you have a large bank balance, without first doing a cash flow analysis. Otherwise, you may find you will just have to put it back in again, when the large monthly bills become due.

Once you establish an average level of profitability for your business over a period of a year or so, you can then begin taking money out at a specific rate, on a regular basis, in line with your average profits. Don't overlook the fact that, for the first year or two, you will probably need to plow a major part of your profits back into the business to build your inventory to more optimal levels, as well as add necessary equipment and fixtures.

Try to resist the temptation to take nickel-and-dime draws frequently or irregularly. These draws are hard to keep track of and you will find, at year's end, that you have taken out more than you realized and cannot remember where it went.

Reducing Self-Employment Taxes

The following advice assumes that your business is a sole proprietorship. If you are a partnership or corporation, different rules may apply, and you should consult your accountant for advice on tax savings.

Let's discuss a few options for taking money out of the business, while minimizing the impact on your profits. One is through payments to a spouse or other family members for work done in support of the business. If, for example, one spouse is employed outside the business and is paying maximum or near maximum Social Security taxes through the outside employer, you can realize substantial savings in taxes by paying the employed spouse for services rendered to the business, instead of taking it out as profit.

The person who runs the business must pay self-employment taxes on the profits of the business. However, payments to a spouse are deducted from profits; thus you reduce the self-employment tax for the person running the business. The spouse receiving the payments must pay Social Security taxes on them, but not if he or she is already paying the maximum.

Beware that you cannot arbitrarily make payments to your spouse just to avoid taxes. Your spouse must be rendering services to the business that are reasonably related to the payments he or she is receiving. See your accountant and the IRS small business tax publications for details.

You are also allowed to pay your children for working at the shop, without deducting taxes, up to a certain amount. Again, check current IRS regulations. This can save you money by transforming allowance money, which you would have to pay anyway, into a deductible business expense. Once again, the pay must be for work actually performed or you will be in trouble with Uncle Sam.

Another option is to set up a simplified employee pension (SEP) plan, through which you can pay a percentage of profits into a tax-deferred IRA. This is fairly easy to do, but payments must be made to all employees at the same percentage that the owner takes. If you have no employees or a small payroll, this can save you some taxes while you are putting away for retirement at the same time. If you have a lot of employees, it may cost more than you can afford. Check with your accountant about how to set up a retirement fund.

Keeping Your Books

When you set up your books, the first decision you will face is whether to use single- or double-entry bookkeeping. The single-entry system is a simplified accounting system, in which each expense or income item is entered only once. The single-entry method is only slightly more complex than your checkbook. The system involves keeping three basic records:

- ◆ Daily cash receipts
- ◆ Monthly cash receipts
- ◆ Monthly cash disbursements

The double-entry system is slightly more complicated, requiring each item to be entered once as a credit and again as a debit. The advantages of this system are uniformity and having a system of checks and balances, which detects errors and minimizes fraud.

You are not required, by the IRS or anyone else, to use a particular bookkeeping system unless your business is very large. This may come as something of a surprise to you because you have probably assumed that Uncle Sam would surely require you to use a system involving complicated paperwork. Given the choice, you can either opt for simplicity with the single-entry system or the checks and balances that flow from the double-entry method. In a small, owner-managed business, you can probably get by without the benefits—and the extra cost and hassle—of the double-entry system. Instead of going into further detail in this book about accounting methods, you can pick up *Small-Time Operator* by Bernard Kamoroff, CPA (Laytonville, CA: Bell Springs Publishing). This is an excellent manual written in plain language for small businesses. It contains samples of all the ledgers and worksheets you need to set up your books, along with clear, easy-to-understand instructions on almost everything you will need to know from a financial standpoint. Accordingly, the rest of this chapter will assume that you have this or a comparable reference, although I will outline other options and methods that you may wish to consider, depending on your unique needs and capabilities. You should engage an accountant to review your accounts before you start, especially if you opt for a double-entry system.

> **Our Experience**
>
> I admit we did not hire an accountant at first and had no problems. Maybe ignorance is bliss! We subsequently had our accountant review our books and he found no problems, although he did suggest some money-saving ideas we had not thought of previously.

Two Essential Financial Reports

There are at least two reports that are important to your business and with which you should be familiar. These are the balance sheet and the profit and loss (P&L) statement. The balance sheet gives you a picture of the net worth of your business. The P&L statement shows your sales, expenses, and profit for a given period. Examples of both these reports are in *Small-Time Operator*, but they do deserve some discussion here.

Balance Sheet

The balance sheet is prepared at the end of the year and shows current assets, other assets, current and long-term liabilities, and your net equity in your business. This is very helpful in dealing with your bank on loans and in establishing one measure of your business's worth if you decide to sell it. The best time to prepare a balance sheet or have your accountant prepare one is when you file your income taxes for the year. A typical balance sheet is shown in Table 19-1.

Balance Sheet XYZ Company For Period Ending December 31, 2004	
ASSETS	
Current cash (change drawer)	$125
Cash in bank	3,879
Accounts receivable	0
Prepaid rent	1,900
Inventory at cost	16,681
Subtotal current assets	$22,585
OTHER ASSETS	
Equipment at cost	$2,788
Less accumulated depreciation	<2,062>
Subtotal other assets	$726
TOTAL ASSETS	$23,311
LIABILITIES	
Current liabilities	
Accounts payable	0
Loans payable	0
Long-term liabilities and loans	0
TOTAL LIABILITIES	0
Net equity in business	$23,311

Table 19-1. Balance Sheet

The example shown is a simplified statement, but it generally reflects the condition of a small business that does not owe any money, that pays its bills on time, and that does not extend direct credit. All of these practices are recommended for a beginning enterprise.

Profit and Loss Statement (P&L)

The P&L statement provides useful information on your sales volume, your expenses, and your bottom line—your net profit. It should also be prepared at least annually, but it is a good idea for you to prepare it more often, monthly at first and at least quarterly thereafter.

These interim reports will likely be only estimates, since it is not easy to exactly establish your "cost of goods sold" entry without a physical inventory, and it is usually not practical to do this on a monthly basis unless you have a very small number of items in inventory. You can, however, estimate this cost by reviewing your inventory records or by multiplying your sales by your historical cost-of-goods percentage, which is calculated by subtracting your markup percentage from 100 percent. Inventory management is discussed in the next chapter.

If you use the keystone markup, your cost of goods will probably vary between 50 percent and 60 percent of sales. You will know your expenses and you can use these figures to calculate your gross profit (gross sales less cost of goods), your total expenses, and your net profit (gross profit less expenses) for each month or quarter. This will be educational—and a little frightening—since your profits will vary significantly, monthly and quarterly. You will probably show losses in some traditionally slow months, such as January. Don't despair—Christmas is coming!

The P&L statement will also enable you to keep an eye on your expenses and take steps to control costs that are getting too high and unduly affecting profitability. Set up your statements to show considerable detail of expenses and compare them with last year's numbers. If you use a computer, your software program, such as Quicken, will generate this report for you and even compare the results with results from previous periods. A sample P&L statement is shown in Table 19-2.

Using the P&L Statement

Using this comparative statement, you can see that although sales were up, so were expenses, causing net profits to increase only

Profit and Loss Statement for XYZ Company For Period Ending December 31, 2013		
	2012	**2013**
Gross sales	$95,000	$115,000
Cost of goods sold	<55,000>	<65,000>
Gross profit	$40,000	$50,000
Expenses		
Advertising	$2,000	$3,500
Car and truck expenses	500	800
Depreciation	600	400
Insurance	500	500
Legal and professional expenses	200	200
Rent	12,000	14,000
Office supplies	2,000	2,500
Taxes	5,000	7,000
Travel	1,500	1,000
Meals and entertainment	500	300
Wages	3,000	4,500
Miscellaneous	1,500	2,500
Utilities	1,500	1,500
Total expenses	$30,800	$38,700
Net profit (gross profit minus total expenses)	**$9,200**	**$11,300**
Profit as percent of gross sales	9.9%	9.8%

Table 19-2. Profit and Loss Statement

a small amount. By scanning the expenses, you can quickly spot those items that increased substantially and perhaps take steps to reduce them.

Your major goal should be to hold the line on expenses, while continuing to increase your sales. Since your gross profit margin will be relatively constant, any increase in sales without a corresponding increase in expenses will result in increased profits.

Most of your expenses, such as rent, utilities, and insurance will be fixed, because you will have to pay these regardless of your sales. Other expenses, such as wages, supplies, and other miscellaneous expenses, will vary with sales, but not in direct proportion. In other words, a doubling of sales will not cause a doubling of these expenses, although they will increase somewhat. This relationship makes sales volume your key tool to increased profits, provided you have adequate pricing policies and good expense controls.

One expense that is almost totally discretionary also has a major impact on sales volume and is a key indicator to check on a profit and loss statement—advertising. Your goal should not be to minimize this expense, but rather to raise it to a level that optimizes your sales volume. This, like much of the other advice in this book, is easier said than done. You will have to experiment with the different advertising media and try to find the ones that bring the most sales.

Computerizing Your Books

If you have a personal computer, you should examine the many accounting packages available for small businesses. However, unless you are well versed in the use of computers and this type of software, setting up and using even a package system may require more time and effort than you can afford to devote to it, given the other demands on your time from your fledgling business. You can always start out manually and switch to a computer after several years in business.

Starting out manually, with a simple system, can be a valuable experience for you and permit you to better understand your business before you attempt to automate it. If you have bookkeeping experience or are intimately familiar with computers and software, by all means, go for it! While automation and efficiency are great, simple may be better, at least in the beginning. However, as your business grows, you will probably find that some sort of computer system is essential for maintaining accurate records within the available time.

Our Experience ● We started out keeping our books manually, but quickly began using our computer increasingly for our records and finances. After reviewing the available software, we purchased Intuit Quicken®, which is basically a checkbook program. Although it is a simple, single-entry system, we found it to be very powerful and more than adequate for our accounting needs. We purchased several of the upgrades to the program as new features were added that we felt we could use. Most of the more complicated accounting packages, including the QuickBooks® package by Intuit, simply have more features—and complications—than a small retail shop owner needs. Most of the more sophisticated reports and analyses available in these packages are simply overkill for a small business such as ours.

Computers and Software

Today, it is virtually impossible to operate a business of any size without eventually becoming involved with that ultimate modern invention, the computer. Quantum advances have been made in hardware and software and the numbers and affordability of computers and software have increased dramatically and will likely continue to do so. Even though it is possible to start your business without a computer, the low prices and variety of software titles today almost compel you to computerize at the start if you are computer literate. If you aren't, you should learn. It is not as scary as most folks believe. Using computers can greatly increase your efficiency and allow you to effectively manage a much larger business than otherwise possible. With the rapid advances in technology, you will be faced with two questions:

◆ Should you buy current models or wait for the next generation?
◆ How often should you upgrade?

As usual, there is not really one answer that fits all situations, but here is one strategy that is sound for a small, startup retail business. First, purchase hardware that is one generation behind; then, skip one or two generations before purchasing an upgrade. The big advantage in doing this is cost, as the older models tend to drop in price as soon as a new microchip is introduced. Not being on the cutting edge of technology is a small price to pay for some significant savings.

So computerize, but don't try to keep up with the latest technology. Pick a machine that will do the job and stick with it for a while, upgrading only when significant new features are available at a reasonable price.

What about software? Again, it depends mainly on your knowledge of standard software varieties, such as spreadsheets and databases. If you cannot use the features of these two types of software, then it is better to choose a software package that has been specifi-

> **Our Experience**
>
> Our first computer had an 8086 processor and a 20-megabyte hard drive. It was slow as cold molasses compared with today's models, but at the time it seemed like lightning. About three years later, we moved up to a 386SX model with a 107-megabyte hard drive, then a 486 machine. It was rendered obsolete with the advent of the Pentium chip, which was the last one we used in our business. We purchased the 8086 machine just when the 286 models came out, the 386SX when the 486 models came out, and the 486 when Pentiums were introduced. I occasionally lamented that my computer was too slow in calculating our monthly inventory, sometimes taking more than two minutes. Susie would respond, "What would you do with an extra two minutes, anyway?" That usually brought me back to reality.

cally designed for retail stores or to have someone custom design a program for you. The only drawbacks of either option are cost and flexibility. Several package programs for retail are very expensive or lack the flexibility to accommodate your particular operation or both. But numerous packages are on the market and it would be a good idea to explore them before you commit to a custom design. For example, some complete systems have been designed for auto, video, hardware, liquor, and other stores, which might fit your needs. You will usually find software vendors at the merchandise shows at major market centers. Talk with several and ask for demo discs so you can evaluate their products before buying.

If you have some database and spreadsheet skills, you can very easily create systems to control your inventory, payroll, word processing, and general administrative chores. If you have considerable knowledge of these basic programs, you might choose to set up your own systems.

You should consider software such as Microsoft Excel®, Microsoft Access®, Microsoft Word®, and Intuit Quicken® as the basics for managing your business, along with some specialty programs for desktop publishing.

Using Excel, you can set up a spreadsheet for each employee that calculates gross pay, withholding, payroll taxes, and net pay by simply entering hours worked. It also calculates the taxes due to the IRS and maintains complete records for preparing the quarterly tax reports and the W-2 forms at year-end.

Checks can be written in the Quicken program. You can set up tables in Access, in which you could enter new merchandise received, items sold at each store, and items ordered. From this basic information you can create reports and screens that display current inventory status and a variety of other information that will help you manage your store, such as:

◆ Monthly inventory list
◆ Weekly list of outstanding orders
◆ Consignor payments due
◆ Year-end inventory list

In addition, a number of useful reports can be produced when needed, such as a best-sellers list (which gives the dollar sales from all items in descending order over any defined period), the inventory value at any time, the value of outstanding orders, and virtually any other information you need to know. You can also use Access to keep your mailing list and print the labels for your newsletters. As mentioned earlier, the Quicken financial program is excellent for money management.

If all this talk about computers is freaking you out, don't despair. You don't have to start out with a computer if it frightens you and you don't have the skills. You can manage effectively without computers, at least until your business has grown to the point that you can master them or until you can afford to hire someone to do it for you. Remember that computers are merely tools for managing more efficiently; they are not ends in themselves. If you can see that they can help you, use them. If not, do it the old-fashioned way until you are convinced a computer would be helpful.

Wrapping It Up

The very best advice is to keep up with your finances on a monthly basis during your first year of operation, no matter which accounting system you use or how you do it. Make sure you use the profit-and-loss report to analyze your operation and to make management decisions to improve your financial position. If you lose track of your finances, you will lose valuable time, during which you could have made corrections. In a small, minimally capitalized business, such a loss of reaction time can be disastrous.

I am convinced that many of the beginning retailers that fail could survive, if they better understood and monitored their finances. One of the more interesting current TV shows to me is *Restaurant Impossible*, on which actual failing restaurant owners use the services of the TV host to analyze, refurbish, and revitalize their businesses. I am amazed that most of the owners do not know what their costs are, and as a result, they are slowly bleeding their businesses to death. Beyond that, most are highly resistant to actually disciplining themselves to see the truth about their finances, preferring to run their operations by the seat of their pants.

While the accounting chores may sound formidable, they are manageable and will become routine if you set up your books carefully and exercise discipline to keep them up on a daily basis. Never fear—you are well able to conquer the accounting monster.

Chapter 20

Managing Inventory

One of the most time-consuming and worrisome tasks you will face in operating a retail store is keeping up with your stock. You will almost certainly have several hundred and possibly several thousand different items in stock. The appropriate business term for all this stuff is inventory (stock is also used interchangeably). It can also be a verb—and a dirty one, at that—when it is time to count all those items.

Establishing an Inventory System

You will probably have a large number of items in your inventory, unless you have a very narrow product mix. You may be able to combine several items from the same vendor under one code if they are the same price and are similar items. For example, you may have stuffed toy bears, cows, and lambs from a single supplier, each priced at $4.50. You can use one code, ABC-1, Stuffed Animal, for all three items. This simplifies inventory, but it limits your ability to correctly appraise the selling potential of the individual items, because they are lumped under one code.

Even after these combinations, you will still likely have 1,500 or more individually coded items with which to deal. This will cause you to spend a significant chunk of time every day tracking inventory. That brings up a good question: Is it worth it? You will discover, by talking with other retailers, that they do not all keep up with their inventory on an ongoing basis. Many simply count everything once a year to establish a cost of goods sold and don't bother with it again until the next tax year ends. Some retailers never count their stock at all, relying instead on estimates to establish the cost of goods.

Since no one is enamored with work for work's sake, you may even consider abandoning an inventory system and only counting once a year. After all, if so many people don't do it, why should you? But one of the hard lessons of entering business is that just because many are doing or not doing a certain thing, it does not automatically make it the correct thing to do or not do. You will find that in retailing, as in life, there are some lazy and ineffective operators who do not bear emulating.

When you are the new kid on the block, it is normal to assume that the old-timers always know the best ways to do things and your tendency will be to copy them. While it is good to have a certain humility and be willing to learn from others, it is a mistake to go against good solid principles and your better judgment, even if "everybody does it."

So, don't automatically assume that your ideas are worse than the next person's. Give yourself credit and follow your good judgment. That is why new businesses sometimes succeed while other, older ones are failing.

Inventory Management Advantages

Keeping a current inventory is worth the effort. You will want to establish and maintain a system for tracking your inventory on a daily basis, unless you are selling only nails, screws, jelly beans, or other items with large numbers and low per-item prices. Although it requires work and discipline to maintain, a good inventory system will make it much easier to meet the needs of your customers—the key to growing a successful business.

Here are some of the advantages of a good inventory tracking system.

Theft control. Without an inventory system, it is impossible to know if you are being ripped off by customers or employees until it is too late. While an atmosphere of trust is the ideal, with no problems with employees and very little shoplifting, it is foolish not to have some safeguards.

Customer service. You can avoid running out of stock constantly and you can determine if an item is in stock and locate it more readily if you keep track. You will be surprised at the number of customers who will ask for an item after it is out of stock and want you to order it for them. Without a good inventory system, you will have a hard time locating an out-of-stock item, price, and manufacturer.

Financial management. Inventory systems help you keep track of how you are doing. Would you fly with an airline that sets a course in New York and doesn't check it again until Los Angeles? It makes just as little sense to go for an entire year without knowing the status of your stock.

Product tracking. An inventory system allows you to keep track of specific items and weed out low sellers. You can spot slow sellers that are taking up space and move them out with sales or markdowns.

Setting Up a System

There are a number of specialized computer software programs available for tracking inventory. Some are relatively inexpensive and deserve a look from you. Many of these packages allow you to print and read bar code labels, print invoices, and provide a complete array of reports and statistics. If you decide to use proprietary software for inventory, you should select it before your goods begin arriving, so that you can enter them into the system properly from the start. Changing systems midstream may not be easy. For instance, most systems require specific coding. Although many will advertise great flexibility, they may not be able to accom-

Our Experience ●

When we started out, we used a paper inventory system, using individual stock records and inventory sheets, as described below. We used an alphanumeric coding, consisting of four letters followed by four numbers. The four letters were usually the initials or the first four letters of the vendor's name, followed by the numbers to identify a particular item from that vendor. This system allowed us to look at a stock number, identify the vendor, and go straight to the stock card and identify the specific product. As we grew, we set up simple databases in Borland Paradox® and later Microsoft Access®, to track inventory and produce reports. We considered and rejected several package programs because we could not find one that would use our coding system. We had become so used to our coding that we did not want to abandon it for a plain number that told us little about the product or manufacturer.

modate another coding system, so you should decide on inventory software before beginning to code items.

One disadvantage of using a package inventory system is the inability to use stock numbers that relate an item to a specific product and vendor. You can always look up the information in the inventory system, but it is not transparent from a stock number and you may not have the time to chase it down when you are waiting on a customer.

You can also use a database program, such as Microsoft Access, to manage your inventory. These programs can handle almost any kind of descriptive product code, but it will require more computer skills to develop than a package system. You will also have to develop your own reports and statistical analyses.

If you are not comfortable starting out with inventory software, you can start out with a single card system and then switch to a computerized system as your store grows. If you opt never to computerize, a card system can still be effective, although it will always have limitations, as compared with computer programs.

Inventory Number:	AS-19
Vendor:	Acrobatic Sales
Vendor Code:	AS
Description:	Teddy Bear
Manufacturer's Stock Number:	665
Minimum Stock Level:	6
Maximum Stock Level:	12
Cost:	$ 9.75
Retail Price:	$19.75

Ordered			Received and Sold			
Date	P.O. #	Quantity	Date	Received	Sold	Balance
1-3-04	1234	8	1-10-96	8		8
			1-11-96		3	5
1-12-04	5678	5	1-19-96	5		10
			1-20-96		5	5

Table 20-1. Stock Record Card

You should purchase 8-by-5-inch, preprinted inventory cards from your office supply store, similar to the stock record card shown in Table 20-1.

These cards have spaces for the item code, description, supplier, cost, selling price, beginning stock, sales, and current balance. They are printed on both sides and each card will normally last for up to a year or more of normal sales.

When a new item arrives, assign a unique inventory code and enter a description, your cost, selling price, and the amount of your beginning stock. A simple coding system is to use alphanumeric codes, with the first one to four digits being an abbreviation of the vendor's name, followed by an item number. For example, items from a company called Homespun Cottage could be coded HC-1, HC-2, and so on.

You have to be careful not to duplicate previous codes because many manufacturers have similar names within an industry. Once you have the card filled out, then file it alphabetically by its inventory code in a card tray.

Your next step is to set up a file for each vendor, where you can keep catalogs, brochures, and invoices. This way, you can go straight from your inventory cards to the vendor's file.

When you sell an item, you put the inventory code on the sales ticket. During the day or at the end of the day, you update the inventory cards from the sales tickets. Obviously, this requires pricing each item individually, with a tag or sticker showing the code. This can be a sizeable task when you receive a large order, but it is worth it. With some small, low-cost items this is impractical, so in that case, you can post the code on the bin or container. These items are usually located near the checkout counter, for convenience and for security purposes.

Even if you use a computer, you can still use the same sales tickets, merchandise coding, daily posting, and pricing systems. The only difference is that you will enter the daily sales and receipts on a computer-generated printout, which you then input into the computer on a periodic basis, such as weekly or monthly. Each week or month, you update the inventory and generate a new printout for the succeeding month.

A handy item to purchase is a pricing gun, which is capable of mechanically printing your price codes on the price stickers. This can greatly improve efficiency in pricing merchandise, especially for multiple items. A pricing gun will also eliminate many errors resulting from misreading different handwriting styles. If you use an alphanumeric inventory coding system, you will find that standard pricing guns may not accommodate your system. However, most companies will make a custom imprint wheel to accommodate your system for a reasonable charge.

If you have started with a computerized inventory system, you should be able to use your computer and the inventory software to print bar-coded labels and read them when an item is sold. The software then makes the needed changes to your inventory.

Managing Your System

Now that you understand the mechanics of the inventory system, you will need to establish some policies and procedures for managing your inventory with the system, whether manual or computerized. Obtaining knowledge about your inventory is useless unless you use this information to improve your store's sales and profitability. Review your inventory on a daily basis as you post sales and watch for these indicators.

Items that are selling well and have low stock balances. With this type of item, you will find it helpful to establish and indicate on the inventory card or computer sheet a desirable reorder point, allowing time for shipping. For example, if you sell an average of two of a certain item per month and it takes a month to reorder and receive a new shipment, then the reorder point would be when you are down to two items in stock—or three, if you want to keep a margin of safety.

Slow sellers that have been in inventory a long time. Unless these are seasonal items, which will sell later, you should consider putting them on sale. Mark them down to move them out so you can put your money into other, faster-moving items. Be brutal here, marking them down until they move, even if you have to take a loss. This is painful, but it must be done!

Hot sellers for which sales have increased. For these items, you should increase your order quantities or put in a special order, to take advantage of the selling surge. You have to strike while the iron is hot!

In addition to your daily checks, you should also thoroughly review all your inventory items at least quarterly, to look for the same indicators mentioned above. Note the poor sellers and use these items as the main attractions in periodic sales.

You do not want to run a continuous sale unless you are in the discount business, but you can plan three or four sales each year to get rid of slow-moving merchandise and to boost sales during slow times of the year. Another option is to periodically maintain a sale table, on which items are placed for quick sale.

Some examples of sales themes you can use for your regular periodic sales are:

◆ After-Christmas sale, during which you sell all unsold Christmas items at half-price, usually lasting only a week or two.

◆ Valentine's Day sale, the week before Valentine's Day, during which you give 10 percent off anything heart-shaped or with a heart on it and also mark down your slow movers.

◆ Gambler's sale, which is a good inventory clearance sale for late summer. During the sale week, mark down your ugly ducklings 10 percent per day, starting on Monday, so that by Saturday, they are 60 percent off. The gambler's sale can stimulate a lot of interest, as customers gamble on when to buy an item at the lowest price without losing it to someone else. Always send out a flier to your mailing list to publicize this sales event, to draw your regular customers. This sale can be a good way to clear out stock before the Christmas season.

These are just three examples of sale themes. Use your imagination and creativity to come up with your own.

When you have a sale, do not group your sale merchandise in one location in the store, except for a sale table of seasonal merchandise. Instead, place brightly colored stickers on the sale items throughout the store. This exposes the sale shoppers to your regular-priced merchandise and encourages them to purchase more than just marked-down items.

Physical Inventory

The final inventory activity you will need to deal with is the annual physical inventory. Despite some merchants' practices to the contrary, the physical inventory is essential to the prudent financial management of your store and should not be skipped. You must do this at the end of your tax year, which is almost always the calendar year. You might close one or two days at year-end, even working on New Year's Day if you don't care that much for football.

There is not much to say here, except that it is a lot of work. To get started, you can make lists from your inventory system before the physical count and use these to make your count. These lists should include the item code, the cost per item, and the inventory quantity shown on the records, along with a space beside each item for the actual count and a space for the total value of that item in stock, as shown in Table 20-2.

Item	Code	Cost per Item	Inventory Quantity	Actual Quantity	Value
Wooden Sign	AA-01	$ 3.50	5	4	$14.00
Teddy Bear	AS-19	9.75	8	7	68.25
Fruit Basket	AT-13	12.50	2	2	25.00
T Kitchen	AT-14	10.00	10	10	100.00
Wreath, Pansy	AT-15	8.50	1	1	8.50
Pillow	BA-09	2.50	2	2	5.00
Angel	CL-03	3.50	2	2	5.00

Table 20-2. End-of-Year Inventory List

After the count, you calculate the value by multiplying the cost times the actual count. This column is then totaled for all items to give the total inventory value. With a manual system, you do this by hand, but a computerized inventory system can calculate the

When we changed from a paper inventory system to a computerized system, we used a laptop computer to enter the codes and quantities as we moved through the store on inventory day. At completion, our database inventory program then sorted and merged the list to instantly calculate current inventory value and update the year-end inventory. We found it easiest to start at one end of the store and move through each section systematically, counting everything as we went.

Our Experience

values, along with differences between actual and recorded inventories. By comparing the actual and calculated inventories, you will have an idea of the loss of goods through theft or disappearance.

Summary

In general, keeping up with your inventory will be a boring, time-consuming activity that you will be tempted to neglect. To do so, however, will be to lose control over one of the key factors to successful retailing and to a profitable, well-managed business. Do so at your peril.

Instead of treating the task as drudgery, try to look at the activity as providing variety to your life. Or, consider inventory tasks as the price you pay for shopping at all these fun and exciting market centers and opening up packages of interesting goodies that arrive at your store periodically. However you look at it, make sure to do the inventory.

Chapter 21

Family and Employee Relationships

Employee Options

Depending on the kind of business you enter, your dealings with others who work with you in your business may consist of supervising your own children as part-time employees; working with your spouse; or recruiting, training, scheduling, and providing daily supervision of a dozen or more people. Each of these employment relationships has unique problems that occur frequently and there are certain principles that apply in all situations. This chapter discusses some of the problems you may encounter with various types of employment relationships.

Employing Your Children

Supervising your own children in your business will involve a degree of pain and suffering that you have experienced many times over.

In addition to working with each other, we have benefited from hiring our teenager and have also employed up to five other employees on a full- and part-time basis. We have, therefore, avoided the major hassles inherent in a large work force.

Employing your offspring is a common practice that seems to offer many advantages but, as in most family matters, may not be as desirable as it appears. Hark back, now, to those days of yester-year, when it took you longer to coax and threaten that youngster into mowing the lawn or cleaning the house than it would have taken to do it yourself. But, as parents, you owed it to the child to teach him or her a lesson in self-discipline and industriousness. Well, you will have some of the same problems with your children working in the business.

You might think that because they are getting paid now and you are not in parent-child roles, but an employer-employee rela-tionship, this will make a difference. But, kids are smart. They know that, despite what you say, you are still good old Mom and Dad and they can still manipulate you as they have done successfully for so many years. So, don't fool yourself that you can eliminate the parental role from the busi-ness relationship. Your chil-dren will not hesitate to ask to leave early to go out with friends, request an advance on next week's wages, or tell you how you should operate the business.

Our Experience ● Our son proved very good at handling money and dealing with customers. This experience allowed him to secure a steady job as a checker for a supermar-ket chain, where he was able to continue his experience in an employee-employer relation-ship that is more realistic and demanding, which is something that is not really possible in the family business. Later on, when he was a junior in college, study-ing radio and TV, he was able to contribute significantly by writ-ing and providing voiceovers for our TV commercials.

These insights should not discourage you from using your children in the business, as it still has many positive aspects. However, you must dispel any illusions you may have about the ability to sep-arate business from family.

The positive aspects of employing your children are:

◆ Enjoying the economic benefit of having your children work for the money they receive from you and being able to deduct their wages from your before-tax business income

- Providing hands-on, valuable job experience and training for your children
- Spending more time together as a family, albeit in the business setting

Spouses and Partnerships

Many small retailers are mom-and-pop operations. While this is not a new thing, the media has recently shown an increased interest in spousal business enterprises. If you plan to extend your marital relationship into the business arena, you will need to consider several issues and establish some ground rules. Even if you are partners with someone other than a spouse or you are in business alone, many of the principles still apply to your relationships with your partner or manager.

The first bit of advice is not to believe that a joint business venture can salvage a shaky marriage. This may seem obvious, but when you consider that couples have children in the hope that a baby will draw them closer and solve marital disputes, it is not unreasonable to assume that some people may believe that a business relationship will do likewise.

This concept is roughly equivalent to a ship's captain deciding that the best way to save a ship that has hit an iceberg is to begin an intensive effort to relocate all the deck chairs and inventory the supplies. It might divert attention from the real problem for a while, but it won't fix it. Sooner or later the boat will sink, albeit with a neat deck and up-to-date inventories.

Therefore, if your marriage has problems, fix them before you engage in activities that will merely divert attention from them. If you cannot function as a team in your personal relationship, it is unlikely you will do any better with the additional dimension of a business relationship.

It also seems prudent not to enter into business together at the same time that you get married, unless you know each other very, very well. Your first couple of years as newlyweds will require many adjustments just to resolve those major issues involving in-laws, finances, sex, and whether the toothpaste tube should be squeezed from the bottom or in the middle. Adding the stress caused by a new business would be unfair to the marriage—and the adjustments to the marriage would be detrimental to the potential for business success.

Another consideration is whether or not both spouses have personality traits that allow them to enjoy, or at least tolerate, a close relationship 24 hours a day. If one or both of you has a need for a lot of psychological space or is basically a loner who requires solitude and distance for long periods of time, a business joint venture may be doomed to failure, or at least may guarantee misery to one or both of you. Some marriages survive in spite of vastly differing personality traits and psychological needs because separate work interests and activities provide a safety valve. Take away the safety valve by combining work and play and you can have an explosion.

Even with these caveats, a spousal business partnership can be a rewarding, fulfilling experience that can strengthen and enrich a marriage. If your marriage is in good shape and you follow some guidelines to minimize conflict, a spousal business venture can be a great idea. Notice that conflict can be minimized, not avoided, since conflict is inevitable when two people live and work closely together. Some rules that serve to reduce friction are described below.

First Rule

The first rule is to decide in advance who will be responsible for what, based on each spouse's individual capabilities. This implies a degree of knowledge, based on a realistic self-assessment, devoid of both egotism and self-deprecation. In other words, don't assume you know and can do everything better and, conversely, don't play the "I'm more humble than you" game. Becoming a successful businessperson requires a healthy self-image!

After the division of labor is made, each spouse must respect the other's responsibility and authority. That is not to imply that there are to be rigid lines that must never be crossed, since it is also important to communicate and consult on important issues and reach a consensus, where possible. But, in the final analysis, the responsible partner's decision must be respected. Otherwise,

Take our case, for example. I am an engineer and, although I am generally outgoing and get along with people well, I am not blessed with a lot of originality and artistic creativity. I am a logical thinker, have considerable experience in financial and personnel management, and am good at organizing and problem solving. In addition, I have passable carpentry and mechanical skills. Susie, on the other hand, is quite creative and skilled at most crafts and needlework. She has an innate talent for tasteful decorating and, like most women, is more closely attuned to feelings and intuition.

Our Experience

Therefore, we divided up the responsibilities such that she was responsible for the displays, the buying of merchandise, and the day-to-day operation of the shop, including customer relations. I set up the books, did the financial accounting, and accompanied Susie on buying trips to keep track of expenditures and act as "gofer" for her—which took some getting used to. Although we occasionally meddled in each other's business—and got our hands slapped—we were pretty successful in maintaining respect for each other's territory.

you will wind up with a lot of tie votes and the decision-making process is stalemated.

Second Rule

The second rule is to not try to impose your own particular style or idiosyncrasies on your partner. Don't insist that everything be done in the same way you would do it. Even though you are working together, you should still allow each other some space and some latitude to work in the way that is most comfortable to your partner.

As mentioned above, I am an organizer, while Susie is more of a free spirit, who tends to concentrate on creative things or customer service at the expense, sometimes, of neatness. Some of our more notable disputes arose when I came bebopping into the store, criticizing the untidy appearance of the checkout desk or the files, usually at the end of a particularly busy day for her.

Our Experience

Our Experience ● After being burned a few times by the resulting flare-ups, I decided that neatness still counts, but it isn't as critical as continuing to live! On the other hand, Susie learned to be more methodical in handling and filing the tax forms and payroll records I used in order to keep up with the financial reporting.

Third Rule

The third rule is to maintain some separateness. That may sound contradictory to marital closeness, but every human being needs some time away to pursue his or her own interests or simply do nothing. You can accomplish this by taking some time away from the shop, separately. Don't insist that you share every waking moment. Too much togetherness can be stifling!

Our Experience ● I had a full- or part-time "other job," so that's how I got away, while Susie took two days off during the week to spend shopping, staying home, or whatever.

Fourth Rule

The fourth rule is to maintain some other mutual interest besides your business. Couples who are in business together often are so wrapped up in it that they are unable to think or talk about anything else. This becomes very boring to friends and family, resulting in isolation of the couple and a narrow lifestyle that is difficult to sustain. So, do something else, preferably together. Join a bowling league, the local symphony society, a neighborhood association, a church, or anything that you both enjoy and are interested in.

Our Experience ● We are both active in our church and Sunday school, which provided us an opportunity for socializing and for putting our religious faith into action through a variety of activities. Try not to allow the business to intrude into this area of your lives. It is not easy at times, since a business can become an all-consuming passion if you are not careful.

Fifth Rule

The fifth rule is to maintain your family relationships as first priority. Tragic results occur when parents allow their business interests to supplant their responsibilities to their children. Children require a considerable amount of time and effort from their parents in order to fulfill their needs for security and guidance, especially during the elementary and adolescent years. If you are not there for them, they will find others who are—and they may not be the best role models.

If you enter business with young children, it is manageable, but it will require commitment and careful planning to be good parents and successful entrepreneurs. You may be old enough to have children and aging parents; this combination can bring a great deal of stress into your lives, in addition to the normal stresses of operating a business.

Think carefully about your life situation in relationship to the timing of your entry into business ownership. Don't become discouraged, but make a commitment to take care of family responsibilities first and factor the necessary extra time and effort into your plans.

> **Our Experience**
>
> We chose to wait until our children were in high school to begin our business. Even then, there were times when we were not able to do a good job both as parents and as businesspeople.

Sixth Rule

The sixth and final rule is to always reserve some time to be together. Remember that marriages require time and attention to maintain good, quality, caring relationships. Don't let your business rob you of your intimacy. You don't necessarily have to exclude business discussions from this shared time. In fact, some of your most meaningful time together may be spent on buying trips, discussing your plans, hopes, and dreams. Speaking of which, it is important to have dreams that you share with your partner, so you should talk about them and be sure you both are pursuing the same goal.

The partnership in which one spouse is longing for millionaire status through continued expansion, while the other assumes a quiet, modest existence in an owner-operated business, is in for trouble when the conflicting dreams are discovered. Spend time together checking out and comparing those dreams, so you can follow them together. While business discussions are OK during your time together, don't neglect time for fun, foolishness, and sex—not necessarily in that order. Remember: Businesses can come and go, but a good marriage is a jewel to care for and treasure.

Couples should consider acquiring insurance on each other to ensure that the business can continue in the absence of one of the partners. This is not a pleasant thought to contemplate, but it is a prudent step to prepare for unforeseen events.

The positives can far outweigh the negatives in husband-and-wife partnerships. Hopefully, if you decide to combine business with matrimony, you will find that your business relationship enhances and complements your personal lives.

Recruiting Employees

You may be tempted to rely totally on yourselves and your family for employees. This is a mistake. Sooner or later, you will find that situations such as illness, vacations, deaths in the family, or just plain fatigue will require the use of outside help. It is better to have someone trained and ready for such an event. If you can have several people available for part-time, on-call employment, so much the better.

If you run a small shop and are normally on the premises much of the time, expect that some customers will always want to deal

> **Our Experience** ● In our case, we chose part-time help from customers who showed interest and potential as employees and trained them over a period of time. We later hired a full-time manager, along with three part-time employees who could operate the shop as well as we could, on a daily basis. We used the part-time employees two or three days a week during most of the year, more during peak seasons.

with you, personally, and will resent having to do business with your employees. This can result in unfair accusations against your employees by customers attempting to force you to pay more attention to them and cater to them. In simple terms, some customers have a need to always deal with the boss because it inflates their egos and, in their minds at least, gives them some special status.

Don't allow them to appeal to your ego by telling you how much better you are than your employees. Resist the temptation to bask in the glow of their praise and say something negative about a valued employee. A good response in such situations is to say something positive about your employee, such as "We have been very pleased with Joe's work. He has been a real asset to our business." While you will probably have to give special attention to such customers, don't let them dominate you and tell you how to run your business and treat your employees.

Training and Communicating with Employees

It is important to communicate your policies and procedures to your employees. That way, when you are not present, you can be assured that the business will be operated in accordance with your philosophy. This is why you should write down your policies and give them to your employees. While you may be able to get away without doing this if you have few employees and work closely with them on a daily basis, it is definitely a necessity if you have more than two or three employees or if you run more than one shift. You should also work with new employees until you are confident of their performance.

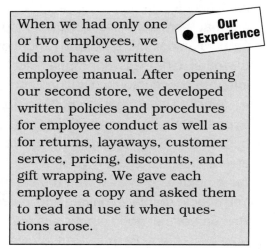

When we had only one or two employees, we did not have a written employee manual. After opening our second store, we developed written policies and procedures for employee conduct as well as for returns, layaways, customer service, pricing, discounts, and gift wrapping. We gave each employee a copy and asked them to read and use it when questions arose.

One particular area that should be emphasized to employees during training, and in your employee manual, is customer service. Everyone has experienced an encounter with an employee who was discourteous, distracted, unavailable, or simply disinterested. Such an experience will discourage customers from returning to your store. Be sure your employees know that they are expected to:

- Greet customers with a smile when they come into the store
- Offer to help, but don't hover
- Avoid personal telephone conversations during work hours
- Dress neatly and appropriately
- Know your stock
- Understand your store policies
- Avoid arguing with customers
- Apologize if they must keep someone waiting
- Avoid profanity and obscenity in speech, even if used by the customer
- Treat the customer as a valued asset, not as a bother or interruption

Complaints about Employees

You will inevitably receive complaints about your employees from some customers. These can be very delicate situations that you must handle carefully. When a customer complains, always remember that there are at least two sides to every story. So, refrain from forming an opinion as to who is right or wrong until you have heard the other side. It is appropriate to assure the customer of your intent to check into the situation and to correct any problems.

When a customer complains about an employee, it is also appropriate to apologize for anything that might have offended the customer and to reinforce your desire that everyone feel comfortable and well-treated in your store. It is inappropriate to summon the employee and deal with the situation in front of the customer. You should do that in private and in a non-threatening atmosphere. Remember that good employees are more valuable than unreasonable customers. Be prepared to give your employee the benefit of the doubt. On the other hand, be prepared to take prompt, firm action to correct inappropriate behavior.

The best way to approach the situation with your employee is to wait for the proper time, simply inform your employee of the customer's complaint, and allow for a response. If you believe the employee acted improperly, try to deal with the behavior and do not attack the employee personally. If it is the first time this behavior has occurred, simply suggest a different, acceptable way of dealing with similar situations in the future. If the same behavior persists, you should continue to discuss performance improvements with the employee and document your directions to him or her in writing, being sure to keep a copy.

Dismissing Employees

If improvement is not forthcoming, you should consider dismissing the employee, again documenting your reasons in writing, for the employee and for your records. If the employee files for unemployment compensation or files a suit or discrimination complaint, it is important to have documentation to defend your actions. This documentation should demonstrate that you informed your employee of unacceptable performance, allowed opportunity for improvement, and provided necessary training in job duties. If time and your budget allows, have your attorney review your proposed action before you take it.

Of course, some offenses warrant immediate dismissal, such as theft, violence, and use of drugs and alcohol on duty. You should have strong evidence of these offenses, however, and document your actions thoroughly. This is a litigious society and more and more employees are suing employers over dismissals and disciplinary actions, so be prepared to defend your actions.

Most states have fairly liberal unemployment compensation laws, but most allow for disqualification of employees who are dismissed for misconduct. Since your business's experience in this regard determines your unemployment tax rate, you should oppose payments to employees dismissed for misconduct. You will be notified when an employee claims benefits and be given an opportunity to appear if you wish to oppose payments. You may be tempted to just let it go, but your tax rate will go up and it will take a long time to get it back to normal. Consult your attorney for specific procedures in your state for opposing a claim.

Employment Laws

You should be aware of the myriad laws and regulations that govern employee work hours, benefits, and treatment. Contact your local labor department office and your state employment agency to obtain specific requirements governing your particular situation. Unless you employ substantial numbers of people, your responsibilities will be relatively simple and easy to fulfill.

Most states will require you to register as an employer with various departments. Check with your business assistance center or labor department to see about registration. You will also have to follow other labor-employment laws and regulations, including those covering:

- ◆ Family and medical leave
- ◆ Workers' compensation insurance
- ◆ Occupational safety and health
- ◆ Wage-hour requirements, such as minimum wage, child labor, overtime pay, and rest and meal periods
- ◆ Antidiscrimination
- ◆ Mandatory posters that need to be displayed at your place of business

Often, the appropriate agencies will find you and get the necessary information to you once you obtain an employer identification number and begin paying taxes to the IRS. But, it is your responsibility to comply with labor laws. The three most important things you absolutely must do to stay in compliance with the law are described below.

Calculate and deduct applicable payroll taxes. First, you must deduct social security, Medicare, and federal income taxes from all employees, regardless of how little or infrequently they work.

Deposit your tax payments and payroll deductions. The second and more important requirement is that you must deposit the taxes deducted from employees, along with your share, on the schedule prescribed by the IRS, which varies according to the amount collected. Check with the IRS for the schedule applicable to your operation. Numerous small businesses are ultimately shut down by the IRS for failure to pay their payroll taxes. Do not neglect this aspect of employee management.

Verify eligibility for employment. The third requirement from Uncle Sam involves completing a form that documents the nationality or immigration status, or both, of all employees.

There is a special form (I–9) that you must complete verifying that you have obtained appropriate identification documents from the employee. Normally you do not submit the forms, but you must maintain them in your files. The Department of Homeland Security and Citizenship and Immigration Services provides an internet-based e-verify service that may be mandatory in your state. Instructions for use are online at www.uscis.gov.

Your state also will probably require you to withhold state income taxes and pay unemployment insurance on all your employees. Just as with the IRS, you must make sure to pay the state revenue department.

You cannot treat occasional workers as "contract labor" and avoid these taxes. Remember all those cabinet nominees presidents Bush and Clinton wanted in their administrations who had to withdraw because of the "nanny" problem? The only people who qualify as contract labor are those who furnish their own tools and work on some basis other than hourly or salary. The bottom line is that retail store workers don't qualify as contract labor.

Principles of Employee Relations

Employee relations can be summed up in a couple of statements.

First, always treat employees with respect, give them the benefit of the doubt, train them properly, and communicate regularly and clearly with them.

Second, provide them the tools they need to do their job, give them a safe, pleasant environment in which to work, and pay them a decent wage.

Don't expect adults with significant skills and experience to run your store in your absence at minimum wage. Check around your area for prevailing wage practices, but don't be overly eager to get by with the minimum. A competent, dependable employee is worth a reasonable wage. You can also give your employees perks, such as discounts of 10 percent to 20 percent off on your merchandise. You might also consider setting up a simplified employee pension (SEP) IRA, and offer group health insurance if it is feasible.

You will experience virtually no problems with your employees if you consider them your friends and equals and treat them as such.

Part 5: Marketing Your Product

Marketing Basics

Marketing for the Small Retailer

Most of us think of Madison Avenue in New York, when we hear the term "marketing." We may associate it with multimillion-dollar corporations, huge ad campaigns, and perhaps sleazy activities. Because of these impressions, one might conclude that marketing is not an activity that could or should be part of a small retailer's business plan.

Before you conclude that marketing is not for you, let's redefine marketing for small retailing purposes. Consider marketing as a plan to present your store and your products to your customers in the most positive and comprehensive manner, in order to maximize your sales, and, more importantly, your profits.

Image and Branding

In an earlier chapter, I recommended that you develop a theme for your store, in order to present a consistent, positive image that promotes customer interest. This process is part of marketing. You should strive to establish your store as a known quantity in your community that is easily recognized and that produces positive feelings in your potential customer base. This is known as branding. While you may not have the resources to establish a national or international brand, e.g., Coca Cola, you can do it locally and among your customer base. You should avoid trying to sell anything and everything to everybody. Try to target a particular segment of the buying public. This can be by income level, marital status, occupation, proximity to your store, special interests or hobbies, or a combination of several of these. Then develop your product line, displays, and image to reach that particular group and avoid abrupt shifts in the types and price range of your merchandise. Here are some ways of accomplishing this:

- ◆ Maintain an attractive storefront and sign.
- ◆ Keep your displays attractive and coordinated.
- ◆ Participate in community activities by sponsoring charitable or school activities.
- ◆ Develop a logo and use it consistently in advertising and promotions.
- ◆ Use consistent and coordinated packaging materials for your merchandise.
- ◆ Establish a price range for most of your merchandise.

Be careful about trying too hard to maintain your image. After you open, you will be besieged by every non-profit agency, school, and booster club to buy advertisements, candy, calendars, and just about everything under the sun. You should establish a budget for these activities and be prepared to say no when your budget is fully committed. As discussed earlier, your logo, packaging, and displays need not be expensive. The important thing is to be consistent.

Advertising Methods

Advertising is probably the most important and expensive part of a retailer's marketing plan and it must be planned deliberately. As mentioned in a previous chapter, you should strongly consider using an advertising agency to help you find your most productive advertising methods. Many large agencies will not be interested in a small retailer's account and, even if they agree to represent you, they may not give you the service you deserve. Try to find a small agency that may just be starting out. These companies will generally work harder for you and provide more personal service.

> **Our Experience**
>
> We were fortunate to find a midsized ad agency through one of its executives who was a customer of our store. She was interested in our merchandise and was always attentive to our needs and respectful of our budget. We provided her with a monthly budget and she procured our advertising, subject to our approval.

Some advertising methods you may wish to try are newspaper, television, radio, hand-distributed fliers, and mail-out advertising supplements shared with neighboring businesses and your own mailing list. Different products and markets demand different advertising methods, so what won't work for one store might be just the ticket for you. Try different methods until you find one that works for you.

One of the most effective advertising media for many small retailers is a newsletter that is mailed or emailed periodically to their own customer mailing list. This has the advantage of targeting people with a known interest in your store, which means the recipient will be more likely to read it, rather than throw it away like junk mail. Newsletters can be produced inexpensively using your own

> **Our Experience**
>
> Shortly after opening, we placed a sign-up sheet in our store, and eventually we had over 7,500 names of customers interested in our merchandise. We prepared our own one-page newsletters, giving information on sales, new merchandise, and ideas for gifts. We used clip art to create some eye appeal. A mailing, though not cheap, always resulted in measurable increases in sales. Later, as the U. S. Postal Service began to increase the cost and logistical requirements for bulk mailings, mailings declined as a profitable advertising medium. The next most effective advertising for us was radio, followed by TV. Billboards were also effective. On the other hand, newspaper advertising and ads in local publications and programs produced lackluster results.

word processing software. They should be brief, informal communications to thank customers for their patronage, inform them about upcoming merchandise arrivals and sales, and tell about new trends in your product line.

Some other marketing methods you should consider include:

◆ Cooperative newsletters with neighboring merchants.

◆ Sponsorship of community events, such as charity races, walks, and rodeos.

◆ Sponsor a local sports team

◆ Purchase an ad on a scoreboard at a local school or stadium

◆ Some of these can be expensive for the small retailer, and may not directly trigger increased sales, but they will help with establishing your name and brand in the community.

Chapter 23 addresses the use of the internet and email as replacements for mail-out advertising.

The Importance of a Marketing Plan

Planning and consistency are factors that are missing in many marketing programs; inconsistency and lack of planning will likely cost you in missed sales. You should develop an advertising program that budgets year-round expenditures. We strongly urge you to begin with such a program, by budgeting a monthly amount for advertising and spending it according to a plan. A suggested starting range for an advertising budget is between 3 percent and 7 percent of your estimated or actual gross sales. Assess results and continue to experiment with changes until you reach an amount that seems to produce optimum levels of sales.

Chapter 23

Marketing
with Email and
Websites

A s discussed elsewhere in this book, maintaining a presence on the internet through a website is considered a must in today's retailing environment. It is a relatively simple and inexpensive process, and if you do not already have one, you should strongly consider it. Chapter 7 gives more information on actually setting up your website and obtaining a domain name, and describes options for maintaining a world wide web presence.

"Snail Mail" vs. Email

Earlier in this book, I discussed the effectiveness of our newsletters, based on a mailing list compiled from in-store customers. Reaching a total of over 7,000 customers, mailing a newsletter never failed to produce an immediate increase in sales. At first, we obtained a bulk mail permit from the post office, had the newsletters printed at a local printer, printed labels ourselves, affixed them to the newsletters, sorted them by zip code, and delivered them to our local post office. All of this was rather simple and inexpensive.

Over the years, however, the U.S. Postal Service has increased both the cost and complexity of using their bulk mail services. The per-unit cost has increased, along with increasingly detailed requirements for labeling, bar coding, sorting, and delivery of sorted mail to centralized bulk mailing centers, instead of a local post office.

Because of these changes, we were forced to use a third party printer who could print and deliver the newsletters to the bulk mailing center. All of these changes increased the cost and time required for a mailing, and pushed us toward reconsideration of the periodic bulk mailings. Although we concluded, at the time, that they were still valuable marketing tools, we did reduce the frequency in order to minimize costs. We also periodically purged our list to eliminate mailings to obsolete addresses. In the late nineties most customers did not have access to email, so there really was not a viable alternative.

As of today, all that has changed. Although there are still some holdouts who do not use email, their number is dwindling rapidly. A large, and growing, majority of households now have access to the internet, making the use of email for customer communication a viable alternative to "snail mail" for small retailers.

Using email has a number of advantages, including the following:

- *Speed.* Notification of the arrival of new merchandise, sales, special promotions, or simply updates on your store can literally be communicated in a matter of seconds.
- *Cost.* There is virtually no cost, after a small setup investment, other than the time to compose the emails.
- *Versatility.* Attachments to emails can include photos and other detailed product descriptions, store policy changes, etc.
- *Targeted advertising.* You can now identify groups of customers who are interested in a particular product or line of products, and provide them information, special sale promotions, etc.
- *Two-way communication.* You can get feedback from customers on a variety of issues, ranging from store hours and product preferences, to store evaluations. People are more likely to check a box on an online survey than they are to mail back a card or tell you face to face.

In short, the days of post office bulk mailings for small retailers may have passed. For the minority of customers who do not have access to email, you may wish to provide hard copies of your newsletters and promotions on a very limited basis. Obviously, if you have very good customers who do not use email, it will be worth your while to keep them informed, even though it is more expensive.

> The last owner of our Austin gift store used email to announce sales, and provide photos of new merchandise, as well as links to the store website where more detailed information and additional photos could be viewed. She offered special discounts on certain days to targeted customer groups, and also announced sales on very specific items in order to move slow-selling items quickly. This was impossible to do with preprinted newsletters.

Our Experience

Using email is not entirely hassle free, especially if you are not computer proficient, but with some outside help, you can develop a low-cost strategy for customer communication that is workable. The advantages of instant, two-way communication with customers and the low cost make this advertising medium a no-brainer!

Remember, email is only viable for existing customers, and does not eliminate the need for a marketing plan to attract new ones, so you should continue to budget for, and execute a media advertising plan, as discussed in Chapter 22.

Blogs

Unless you have been living in a remote cave, you have heard a lot in the recent past about "blogs." They are the latest thing in news and information, especially in the political arena. The term is an acronym (actually, it's a *portmanteau*, or blend of words) for "web logs," which are internet websites that provide a continuing thread of information, opinion, ego-centered propaganda, and sometimes outright lies. Hopefully you will not want to venture into the latter arenas, but blogs do provide an additional way to communicate with your customers and build relationships with them on a continuing basis.

For example, you could use your blog to communicate your market plans, orders that have been placed, expected arrival dates for new merchandise, as well as more personal information on store employees, day-to-day store activities, and the like. While not every customer will want to know about your new shop curtains or wallpaper, some will, and will come in to check them out, thus providing a sales opportunity.

> **Our Experience** ● When one of our friends, who is the owner of a gift store, decided to move to a new shopping center nearby, she set up a blog on her website to provide updates on the progress of the move, including plans, setbacks, and new store layout. She has received a lot of positive feedback from customers who followed the progress on her blog.

Online Forums and Message Boards

Up to this point, this chapter has focused on the marketing aspects of internet use by small retailers. There is an added benefit to store owners being online. When we first started our business, we formed friendships with several store owners in other cities, most of whom we met at market shows. It was very valuable to compare notes with them to see what had worked for them, and discuss mutual problems, even if only to commiserate about problem customers, poor deliveries, etc.

Unfortunately, we only saw them at market shows two or three times a year, although we sometimes kept in touch by telephone. By using the specialized message boards and forums available on the internet, store owners can now form virtual friendships with hundreds of other own-

> **Our Experience** ● A store owner we know has established a circle of contacts in a retailing forum, who she calls her "imaginary friends." She discusses products, sales techniques, and plans market trips with them. She often meets them at gift shows, and has formed "real" instead of "imaginary" friendships with many of them.

ers across the country and internationally. These forums provide a medium to exchange ideas, compare notes, and generally stay abreast of techniques and methods that are working for others.

In the words of Bob Dylan's song, "the times, they are a changin'." Changes that took centuries and decades are now occurring in years and even days. The opportunities for marketing and communication on the internet have increased at warp speed since the beginning of the 21st century, and retailers should take advantage of them to increase their sales and profits. Notable among them are social networking sites such as Facebook, Twitter, and Pinterest, which offer means for promoting your store and its products to a network of friends, acquaintances, and strangers.

Part 6: Planning for the Future

Chapter 24

Managing Change in Your Operating Environment

W e've all heard the many platitudes and adages about change, such as "The only constant in life is change." However, most of us spend too much time talking about and lamenting change rather than actually anticipating, planning for, and embracing it.

Human Tendencies

Psychologists tell us that humans have several basic needs, one of which is security. Most of us find security in repetition and routine. In other words, we like things to stay the same so we can become comfortable with them, and be able to feel secure in knowing that we will be able to deal with them.

If you doubt that people like routine and sameness, try presenting a ten dollar bill to pay a tab of $9.53 at your local fast food restaurant, and after the cashier has rung up the sale, give him or her three pennies, so you will get two quarters back instead of mixed change and pennies. Watch the expression on his or her face. It will likely be one of panic, or at least chagrin, since employees at these places are trained to rely on the register to calculate the change amount, and most are totally unprepared to make change on their own.

While this is a trivial example, it is representative of our aversion to unknown and changing situations in our lives. Remember the definition of inertia in physics? It is the tendency of an object to remain in its present state, absent some outside force. I think that definition fits the human situation with regard to change. We will continue in our present course of living, business operation, and personal relations, unless something forces us to change. While this is not all bad for some areas of our lives, in retailing it can sound the death knell for our business. We mentioned the corner video stores earlier. Do you know of any that have survived the onslaught of Blockbuster and Netflix, unless they have been able to change focus by identifying a niche market, such as a resort location?

Pull of the Status Quo

Let's consider two buggy whip companies in the year 1890. Both decided to develop a mission statement for their companies. The first one developed a mission statement that read: "To make the best buggy whip available and sell it at a reasonable price." The second company's mission statement was: "Earn maximum profits through the manufacture and sale of products that facilitate the transportation of people and goods." Which one do you think had the best chance of surviving after the invention of the automobile? Obviously the second! Why? Because it was focused on the broader goal of earning a profit, while the first company was focused on the product.

Unfortunately, many retailers fail, or at least fail to flourish, because they become married to their product, or to doing business the same way they have always done it. Remember, unless you are independently wealthy, you are in business to make a profit, not to sell widget A, at a particular location, in a particular way! If you do not make a profit, you are history! Failure to anticipate and adapt to changes affecting your operation, will likely send your business to the scrap heap.

Paradigm Shifts

A paradigm is simply a pattern for doing things. It is good to have them, since they allow us to perform efficiently; that is why you should set up standard operating procedures and have an employee manual. But, you should also be aware that paradigms can and must change, in response to changing conditions. Sometimes the changes, or paradigm shifts, are dramatic and sudden, as in the Great Depression, when World War II started, and on September 11, 2001. Our world changed, and literally forced us to change our ways. Other shifts are less dramatic and more evolutionary, as with the changes brought about by the internet, advancing technology, and the changing demands of consumers.

Thinking Creatively

Historians have said that Frederick William II, the Great, of Prussia, lost the battle of Jena to Napoleon in 1806, even though Frederick died years earlier. Prussia lost because the Prussian generals continued to use Frederick's battle strategies, while Napoleon developed new, superior ones.

The parallel to retailing is clear: You can't sell yesterday's products using yesterday's methods to today's consumers.

Sometimes, an old, inefficient method of doing something can hamper efficiency for generations. The QWERTY keyboard, originally developed to prevent interference of typewriter keys with each other, is still used on computer keyboards, even though there are no actual keys to collide, and despite the awkwardness of typing on it.

While there is little you can do to anticipate cataclysmic changes, such as 9/11/2001, you can plan for and adapt to the more evolutionary changes that are inevitable in the retail industry. You may not be able to actually foresee the changes, but you can place your business in a position to react to them as they occur. Some suggestions for making your business more adaptable, or agile, are:

- Avoid viewing the future in terms of your past frames of reference—try to see things from another perspective, i.e. from your customers' viewpoint.
- Keep up with changing technology. You don't have to be cutting edge, but you'd better not be dull, either.
- Focus on your real objective, making a profit, instead of your products or current operating mode.
- Read the business and lifestyle sections of your daily newspaper every day. Don't limit your interest to retailing, per se, keep up with economic and cultural trends.
- Don't invest too heavily in fixed equipment or hardware that is tied to particular products.
- Be open to new products and opportunities.

Expecting the Unexpected

I will end this chapter with this cautionary note.

Roger von Oech, a noted author on creativity, tells a story of an ancient walled city that was under siege. Food was essentially gone, and the city ruler, in desperation, ordered their last remaining food, a large ox, thrown over the city wall onto the besiegers. The commander of the attacking army ordered a retreat, thinking that, if the city dwellers would throw an ox over the wall, they must have a plentiful food supply and wouldn't be surrendering any time soon. The city ruler had done the unexpected, and the army was fooled.

The moral for retailers; unexpected things happen all the time, so don't be fooled. Expect the unexpected, and be prepared to act on proven facts, but don't be fooled by passing fads.

Certainly you must be prepared to react to change, and to unexpected situations, but don't do so rashly or prematurely. Take the time to analyze the situation, discover the real facts, and be slow to abandon your plans. Every wave of change is not substantive, and will not last.

When dealing with changing environments, an old adage comes to mind, as a good rule of thumb. "Be not the first to try the new, nor the last to lay the old aside."

Chapter 25

Protecting Your Store from Internet Competition

O ther portions of this book have discussed the internet, e-tailing, setting up websites, and the evolution of the internet and its impacts on retailing. This chapter will look at ways to determine the degree of competition you can expect from online retailers, and will assist you in choosing or changing your product lines to avoid unnecessary vulnerability. We will examine five different characteristics of products that influence their vulnerability to online competition.

Utilitarian or Decorative?

In general, the more utilitarian or standardized a product, the easier it is to find and purchase it online. Earlier in this book we cautioned against trying to compete with big box retailers on electronics and other standardized products. The same cautions apply to online competition. It is quite easy to go to a site, such as Amazon.com, find and purchase a new X-box game, because they are standardized and used in exactly the same way. You can order it and expect to receive it promptly. If you need a new can opener, the same principles apply, and you may opt for online purchase.

On the other hand, if you are looking for an electronic game that you may only play a few times, and which you may wish to trade in for a different one in a few days or weeks, you would probably opt for a local "Game Exchange" retailer rather than go through the hassle of returning items every time you want to try a new one. Some consumers just will not spend the time and effort to plan ahead, even a few days or hours.

If you want a new braided rug to match the color of your drapes, and fit in a confined space, you may have difficulty finding one online, and even if you found an apparent match, you may not be confident enough to risk ordering it without actually seeing it up close and, perhaps, taking it home to compare colors in reality.

So, if you try to pick products that are more one-of-a-kind, decorative in nature, or which carry a larger risk of varying from descriptions and photos viewed online, you will reduce your vulnerability to online competition.

Size and Personal Fit

Some things just must be tried on before you buy. Online sites can offer color photos, standard sizing, and money back guarantees, but many people are reluctant to commit without actually seeing and trying some things on for size. In shoes and clothes, for example, sizes, though supposedly standardized, actually vary.

Prom, wedding, and party dresses are also items more likely to be purchased locally because correct size and fit, as well as color coordination, are essential.

Using another definition of size, large bulky items are less likely to be bought online, because of the inconvenience and cost of shipping. Most furniture is bought locally, because it can be delivered conveniently by a local store and usually won't require assembly, like many internet/mail order furniture items.

The implications for you, the retailer, are to choose products that are subject to individual sizing and fit rather than products where "one size fits all" is the norm. Also you might consider products that are difficult and costly to ship from a distant location.

Time Sensitivity

Have you ever had a need for something and you needed it right now? We all can identify with this situation, and this is another criterion to evaluate before choosing products for sale in a retail store. I am a do-it-yourselfer, and I have never ordered nails or sandpaper online, because I need them when I need them, not tomorrow or next week. Now, I might get them at Home Depot, if one is available, rather than the local hardware store, so this cannot be the only criterion.

> **Our Experience**
>
> I can usually order shirts and shoes successfully online; I guess my feet and body structure are pretty close to norms. Susie, however, has a terrible time finding shoes and clothes that fit, even though sizing is the same. As a result, she has had to send back items multiple times, with the resulting delays and increased shipping costs, often never finding the right fit. Maybe it's a gender thing, also. Women seem to be pickier than men, as we are more apt to accept items that don't quite fit, rather than go to the trouble of sending them back.

Buying a new dress for an unexpected date is a purchase that must usually be made locally, because time is of the essence.

Seldom do people purchase a piece of homemade fudge from an online source, simply because we don't want to delay gratification for several days, when we may be out of the mood. This applies to a variety of impulse items, although, again, you need to avoid items normally carried by your local mega-mart.

Choosing products that are required in a short time, or are subject to impulse buying, will minimize online competition.

Price Point

In general, very low and very high priced items are not as readily purchased online, leaving the local retailer with a couple of extreme price niches to fill. Sewing notions, small jewelry items, small gift items, as well as expensive furniture, jewelry, and machinery are likely to be purchased on-site rather than ordered.

Gift or Personal Use?

Many people find it convenient to order generic gifts for friends and relatives in distant towns online, because of the convenience. Others prefer to buy locally, especially for very personal gifts, in order to allow for convenient exchange of gifts by the recipient, if needed. There is no general rule of thumb here. You should evaluate products individually to assess the probability of online competition. Some of the factors discussed above will influence this category, e.g., timeliness, size, fit, as well as the uniqueness of the item. Your location will also be important.

If you operate a souvenir shop at a resort, you can probably feel confident that your transient customers will not use an online store to buy tee shirts for family and friends. Conversely, if you operate a store in a remote mining town, with a highly mobile, transplanted population, you might assume that many gifts will be ordered online for direct shipment to relatives and friends back home.

Combined Evaluation

The above factors may be important competition considerations individually, but they are more important in combination with others in the group. For example, handmade dresses that are sold at a resort gift shop are highly unlikely to be vulnerable to internet competition because of the location, personal purchase likelihood, and the sizing requirement.

Conversely, large pieces of expensive furniture may not be a good bet, if you are unable to stock and/or deliver them as fast as an internet supplier.

In the final analysis, there is no sure way to eliminate internet competition, and if there was one now, it would likely change as online retailers improve and innovate. The best you can do is continually evaluate your products, measure sales trends, listen to your customers, and be prepared to adapt to changing market conditions.

Your best weapon against internet competition is your ability and willingness to provide service to your customers that they cannot get online. These include knowing their shopping preferences and catering to them, providing personalized in-home consultation, allowing goods to be taken home on trial, same-day delivery, layaway, and distinctive gift wrapping.

Chapter 26

Selling or Closing Your Business

While some people think retail store owners must be prosperous and make lots of money, retailers know differently. In fact, most retailers will tell you that the only times you come into substantial money is when you sell your store, if indeed you are able to do so, and when you close your doors.

Is Your Business Marketable?

Let's assume you've been in business for several years, you've made reasonable profits, and you want to retire or move on to a different challenge. You consider selling your business.

The first thing you should consider is an often-overlooked threshold question that must be answered: Is your business marketable? Most owners react with surprise and chagrin at this question, thinking something like "Of course it is! I've put my heart and soul into this business, and it is worth a lot!" Even though that may be the case, it does not guarantee that someone else is willing to put out his or her hard-earned money to take it over. Several factors can influence the salability of a business. Here are some aspects worth evaluating, whether you're selling or buying.

Location. Is your store located in a neighborhood that is declining, becoming crime-ridden, or viewed as unsafe? Is it located near an undesirable facility, such as a new highway, a landfill, or a meat processing plant? If so, potential buyers may be reluctant to invest in it.

Profitability. While you may have been making a living from it, would a new buyer have any more or less difficulty in doing the same? (See more about this under "Establishing the Price," later in this chapter.)

Product line. Is your product line appealing to an inclining or declining market share? For example, a retailer of baby products might be in trouble in an area with a declining birth rate.

Competitors. Are other like businesses available for sale or going in nearby?

Startup ease. How difficult would it be for another person to start up a business like yours from scratch?

Intangibles. Do you have substantial intangible assets such as a large mailing list, an established customer base, or a good reputation in the community?

The answers to these questions will indicate the likelihood of your business selling and whether you can derive a premium price or have to settle for something less. If your most realistic option is to sell out your inventory and shut down, you will want to claim as much profit as possible when doing so.

Tips for Closing Your Business

The best strategy for closing out is to quit buying and quietly sell down your inventory over a short period of time, say two or three months, then announce a "going out of business" sale over a period of a week or two at most, with graduated reductions in prices each day. In this way you will maximize the sale of merchandise at full or near-full markup and perhaps wind up with a gross overall profit margin of 50 percent or so on your remaining inventory. If you have a lease, be sure to plan your closing to coincide with the end of your lease or negotiate a lease cancellation prior to closing. Otherwise, you could be stuck paying for the remainder of the unexpired lease term.

> **● Our Experience**
>
> In 1998, we decided to close one of our retail stores in Austin, Texas. We were located in a high-end strip center that had set a goal of almost exclusive occupancy by national retailing chains. As a result, lease amounts were increasing rapidly and our profitability was dropping. Because we wanted to retain our other store in Austin with the same name, we decided in the summer of 1997 to close after Christmas. We negotiated a month-to-month extension of our lease, which ended in August of that year. We placed no orders for merchandise to be delivered after Christmas and sold down our stock during January 1998. At the end of the month, we announced a "store closing" sale during the first week in February; we discounted prices 30 percent on the first day of the sale and an additional 10 percent each successive day. By the end of the week, we were essentially bare. The few remaining items we donated to charity or moved to our other store. Using this method, we were able to achieve an overall gross profit of about 50 percent on our remaining merchandise.

If you decide to close, there is another option to consider. There are a number of specialized businesses that, for a fee, run going-out-of-business sales for retailers who are quitting business. If your operation is large or you anticipate difficulty in selling your stock, you may want to contact one of these brokers to see if their services work for you. If you have been in business for any length of time, you have probably received a solicitation from one of them. If not, try searching on the internet for "business sale brokers."

Setting Up the Sale

If you conclude that your store can indeed be sold, you can proceed to answer the following questions:

- ◆ Is there any urgency in completing the sale?
- ◆ How can you best accomplish the sale?
- ◆ Who would be interested in your business?
- ◆ How much can you get for it?

Timing the Sale

First, let's examine the matter of timing because it can affect your decision as to whether to sell the business yourself or to use a broker. Do you need to sell in a hurry due to health, relocation, or other time-sensitive situations, or can you tolerate a longer process with no deadline? If the former, you may wish to use a broker rather than face the uncertainty of a long, drawn-out process of marketing it to one person at a time. You can always advertise the sale yourself, but you will then have to sort through the crowd of "lookers" and try to focus on the serious inquiries. Of course, using a broker does not guarantee a quick sale, but it will maximize exposure to the greatest number of potential buyers in the shortest time.

Selling It Yourself

Now let's look at the question of how. There are two basic options—do it yourself or use a commercial realtor. Each has its own advantages and disadvantages.

If you opt to sell it yourself, you will have the most control over the process and will be able to target your efforts to people that you believe may have the most potential interest in your business. If you are successful, you will also save the broker's fee, which can be up to 10 percent of the sale price. Selling it yourself also allows you to decide to whom and when to disclose your intentions. It is usually to your advantage to keep your intention to sell confidential, so customers and employees will not be upset at the prospect and begin drifting away. The disadvantages are that your market may be limited, you may not have the resources to publicize the sale, and you must handle all the showing, negotiating, and legalities of the sale.

Who might be interested in buying your business? There are as many answers to this question as there are businesses, but there are some general categories that can help you narrow the search. They are, in the order in which I suggest approaching them:

- ◆ Family members
- ◆ Employees

- ◆ Friends and acquaintances
- ◆ Customers
- ◆ Retirees looking for a second income
- ◆ Refugees from corporate America or crime-ridden or urbanized areas looking for a simpler or more fulfilling lifestyle

If you elect to list with a broker, you will not need to worry much about this subject because your broker presumably has his or her own marketing strategy and pool of potential buyers. If you choose to try to sell your business yourself, then attention to these potential customer categories may expedite the sale.

First, look within your family for a potential buyer. While selling to a family member has the potential for creating long-term family conflicts and division, it deserves some consideration. Perhaps you have a child, grandchild, or other relative who has learned the business and has shown an interest in it. If you are inclined to do so, you may be able to pass the business along with payments structured over a long period of time, thus giving someone a start in business he or she otherwise could not afford.

If you need cash immediately, this may not be possible. In any event, if you decide on this route, be sure to structure the deal in writing, spelling out a clear understanding of the rights and obligations of both parties. This will minimize, if not eliminate, the potential for family feuding later on.

The next most fertile field for locating buyers is your employees. You may have employees who, like family members, have learned the business and have been promoted to managerial positions. If so inclined, these employees might make excellent entrepreneurs. Starting with an established customer base and product line, there may be one or more who could continue to grow your business as their own.

Be careful when approaching your employees. It is best to approach them one at a time while you are determining their interest. Make it clear to each one that your proposal is confidential and they should not pass the information on to other employees or customers.

> **Our Experience** ● In 1999 Susie and I decided to relocate to Harrison, Arkansas, where we started a new retail gift store, along with a bed-and-breakfast. After a year of operating our remaining Austin, Texas, store, we decided to sell it due to the additional work of operating it long distance. We had a very capable manager who had operated the store semi-independently for more than five years. Since we had no family members who were interested in taking it over, we decided to offer her the opportunity to purchase the store. She decided to accept the offer and the purchase was completed in May 2000.

After exhausting these two possibilities, then proceed down the list, identifying potential buyers and approaching them in a manner similar to employees. The "retirees and refugees" can be reached through advertisements in magazines and periodicals that cater to these groups. Some examples are publications by AARP (known as the American Association of Retired Persons until 1999); magazines such as *Money, Entrepreneur,* and *Mother Earth News;* and regional magazines such as *Southern Living.* Be sure to check the internet as a possible advertising medium. There is a myriad of special interest forums and classified listing sites available.

Listing with a Broker

If you decide to use a broker, check out the classified ads in your local newspaper's "Businesses for Sale" classifieds and try to identify one that has listings for businesses similar to yours. Talk to your accountant and banker to try to identify firms with successful track records. After narrowing down the field, ask a few firms to submit references on previous sales similar to yours and then contact those former owners.

Commercial realtors offer the advantages of marketing expertise, help in valuing your business, and a ready pool of potential buyers. Also, they can relieve you of the burden of showing the property and negotiating the deal. Many brokers participate in national networks that can publicize your business all over the country. A significant number of business buyers are people from a different region who have an interest in relocating to your area. You may be unable to tap this pool of potential buyers on your own.

Some disadvantages are that you must usually sign an exclusive sales agreement with the realtor for 90 days to six months. If the broker is unproductive or is not pushing your business satisfactorily, you may have to wait a considerable length of time before you can change agents or sell it yourself. If you list with a broker, you must also give up some control over the confidentiality of your proposed sale. Although most brokers attempt to reveal specifics only to serious prospects, the potential for compromise of confidentiality increases with the number of people who are aware of the proposed sale.

Establishing the Price

The final question to be answered is how much should you get for your business? Here is where it becomes very difficult to be objective.

After all, you gave birth to your business, developed it, and nurtured it along through ups and downs. It is very much your "baby." And who doesn't think his or her baby is the best, brightest, and most valuable thing in the world? But what about other people's babies? Come on, admit it—you have seen some babies that were, well . . . unattractive! The point is, beauty and value are in the eyes of the beholder, and your relationship to your business can destroy your objectivity. That is why you must step back from your business and evaluate it as an outsider, specifically a potential buyer. Ask yourself these questions:

- ◆ Why would anyone else pay money for my business?
- ◆ How much would they be willing to pay?

While there are a lot of complicated formulas available for valuing a business, they all boil down to two basic approaches.

Cost Basis

The first approach is to value the business on the basis of the value of its net assets. For example, for a retail business, you would value the inventory (normally based on cost) and add in the market value of your fixtures, buildings, and any other tangible assets. Then you would try to place a hard-dollar value on intangible assets, such as goodwill, name recognition, customer base, and customer data-bases, such as mailing lists, and then deduct any liabilities. Then you might even add a percentage for your profit.

Disadvantage of Cost Basis

This approach develops a selling price for your business in the same way you establish the selling price of an item of merchandise. Intuitively, this seems like a good way to do it, but it overlooks one critical element: the earning potential of your business. Without considering this critical element, cost basis may not be a good way to place a value on your business because it could result in a price that's unfair, either to you or to the buyer.

Let's examine this potential further. Suppose you have an inventory of $60,000, fixtures worth $10,000, and intangible assets you believe are worth $20,000 and you have no liabilities. Using the cost method, you might expect to sell for about $100,000—cost plus $10,000 profit. Further suppose that your business is generating only $5,000 per year in profits. If you were a potential buyer, would you be willing to invest $100,000 in a venture that is not a sure thing for an annual return of $5,000 or 5 percent? Probably not.

Now, let's look at the value from another point of view. Suppose the cost figures are the same, but your business is regularly producing a profit of $50,000 per year. In this case, the buyer would have a return of 50 percent, but you would be selling at too great a loss! You would never be able to replicate that kind of return on your investment.

Return on Investment Method

To value your business using the return on investment method recognizes there are many options for investing money. You can invest your money in savings accounts or certificates of deposit that provide a return of between 1 percent and 7 percent or you can buy stocks or bonds and, normally, expect rates of return between 6 percent and 25 percent. Also, you could go to Las Vegas or play the lottery, where returns can be as high as 1,000,000 percent or losses could reduce your capital to zero in a heartbeat.

The reason for the differences in the returns on these investments is the level of risk. The savings account and CDs are guaranteed by the government and are virtually risk-free, but their returns are low. Stocks and bonds produce higher rates of return, but with increased risks. And you know that you have a greater chance of getting struck by lightning than winning big in Las Vegas or in your state lottery.

This leads us back to the basic considerations in this second method of valuing your business: return on investment and risk. The rate of return expected by an investor is directly related to the risk assumed. If you invest in a highly volatile stock or mutual fund, where the risk of losing money is high, then you are likely to expect a higher rate of return for risking your money. Conversely, if your investment is risk-free or very low in risk, you will be more willing to accept a lower rate of return.

Determining Risk vs. Return

How do you determine the risk of buying your business?

First, retailers must accept the facts of life that about half of all retail *stores* fail within two or three years. "But," you say, "I've been in business for 20 years." You're right; that is a good indication of stability, which tends to lower the risk. Many other factors also influence the risk, including the historical record of profit growth (or decline), the location of your business, product line stability, and customer base.

Despite low profits, a relatively new business that seems to have potential for growth—with some effort on the part of the buyer—might carry an expectation of a 30 percent, 40 percent, or even 50 percent rate of return. A ten-year-old business that has shown steady profit growth and has a good product line and location might justify a rate of return of as little as 15 percent to 20 percent.

Because of the inherent risk in small businesses, rates of return below 15 percent might not seem to be justifiable in the current market. Historic performance of common stocks—producing returns of 8 percent to 20 percent—has raised the bar for business investment rates of return. After all, investors reason, why should they take on the headaches of running a business when they can put their money into stocks and reap a 20 percent profit without lifting a finger? You might benefit from reminding a prospect that long-term stock market returns are more in the neighborhood of 8 percent to 10 percent.

To use this method of valuing a business, begin with the record of profits for your business, rather than with the cost of your assets. Instead of using your last year's profit, average your profits for the last five years or so.

To examine the two profit scenarios using the example above, we will keep costs the same and assume this is a long-term, stable business with a good location. With this level of risk, we assume that a rate of return of 20 percent is justified. If average annual profits are $5,000, then a selling price of $25,000 ($5,000 / 0.20) is justified. For average profits of $50,000, the selling price would be $250,000 ($50,000 / 0.20). Quite a difference! In the first case, the price would be less than the actual cost of the inventory and fixtures, while in the second case, the price would be twice the total cost value.

Determining an Equivalent Return

One other caveat is in order. Many retailers who actively manage their businesses do not pay themselves a regular salary, but irregularly draw profits from the business. Using the return on investment method described above, a new owner should be able to realize his or her rate of return without actively managing the business in order to have a return comparable to passive investments in a bank or the stock market. To compensate for your managerial services to your business, before applying the formula, you should reduce total profits by an amount equal to the cost that the new owner would incur to hire a full-time manager. For example, if average profits were $50,000 per year, but you were a full-time manager and did not receive a salary, you should deduct the annual cost for a full-time manager, say $30,000, from the total profits, result-

> **Our Experience**
>
> When we sold our Austin, Texas, store to our manager in 2000, we used this method to establish a fair price. We also compared the proposed price with the potential profit if we simply closed the store. Since the totals were approximately equal, we opted to sell.

ing in adjusted profits of $20,000 and a selling price of $100,000 ($20,000 / 0.20).

A Bitter Pill

This return on investment approach is a hard one for most business owners to swallow, but many knowledgeable people believe it is the most realistic method of business valuation. If you are considering selling your business, then it behooves you to get those profits up and keep them up for several years. If, after you apply the rate of return formula, the result is less than your current cost of merchandise and fixtures, you should probably consider selling out your stock and fixtures and closing instead of trying to sell the business.

Good News

As mentioned earlier, the increase in the value of merchandise that you have in inventory is considered income by the IRS and is subject to tax in the year the increase occurs. That is why you can have a cash flow crunch in your first year in business. You expend money to purchase your initial inventory and build it up to acceptable levels. Because much of this inventory must be carried forward to the next year, you receive no income from it, but it constitutes an asset—a paper profit.

When you sell your business or close it, this prepaid tax works to your advantage. As you deplete your inventory to zero, the inventory reduction becomes a deductible cost of goods, which reduces your taxes. So, if you are able to sell your business or sell off your assets, you may reap a sizable sum of money, much of which is not taxable. Please understand that this is a gross over-simplification. You should always consult with a certified public accountant or an attorney prior to selling a business.

Glossary

Assets. These are the items of value that your business owns, such as property, equipment, cash, and accounts receivable. They can also include such intangibles as trade names, goodwill, and mailing lists.

Balance sheet. A financial report that lists the assets, liabilities, and net worth of your business.

Cash flow. The movement of cash, checks, and negotiable instruments into and out of your bank account at a given time or period of time. If it is positive, you have enough money to pay bills, and if negative, you don't.

COD. Literally, cash on delivery. Frequently these are the terms of your first order from a new vendor, and for some manufacturers, all orders. Payment includes not only the cost of goods and shipping costs, but also an additional fee for processing the transaction. This latter fee is called the COD charge.

Collateral. Something of value you are required to pledge as security for a loan and that is generally required to obtain credit at a bank, unless the banker is your mother.

Consignment. The process of taking goods for sale in your store, without paying for them until sold. They remain the property of the consignor until sold, at which time an agreed-upon percentage of the total selling price is retained by the store, with the remainder paid to the consignor.

Cost of goods. A technical term for the cost of purchasing or manufacturing the items you sell. Includes freight costs but not expenses such as rent, utilities, and office supplies. Consult IRS Publication 334 for a detailed definition.

Double-entry bookkeeping. A system of keeping up with your finances involving the entry of each expense and income as a debit and a credit. The system was most likely designed by accountants to confuse mere mortals, and require that you hire them to keep your books. The system does provide checks and balances to detect errors and minimize fraud and deception.

Draw. A term meaning to take money out of your business as profit or payment to yourself if you are the sole proprietor. It also includes the value of merchandise you remove for your own use.

Employer identification number (EIN). An IRS-assigned number you must obtain before employing other persons in your business. Used by Uncle Sam to make sure you pay the required payroll taxes and withhold income taxes from your employees' wages.

Entrepreneur. One who endeavors to provide a service or product to others for a profit. Involves risk and, often, innovative approaches.

Escrow. An account set up to collect and disburse funds for a particular purpose. It identifies the funds and maintains a sufficient balance to make payments, when due. Often used to maintain sales and payroll taxes in a separate account to ensure they don't get lost in your overall bank balance.

Expenses. These are the so-called overhead costs of operating your business, as distinguished from cost of goods, as defined above. Includes such items as employee wages, postage, rent, insurance, and all other ongoing costs of remaining open for business.

Finish-out. The structural, mechanical, electrical, and decorating cost of transforming new or previously occupied retail space into a finished state. The lessor normally provides an allowance for you or them to perform this work.

Gross profit. Gross sales, less the cost of goods.

Inventory. As a noun, this means all of your store's stock that is intended for resale, or the value of same. As a verb, the act of counting and costing your business's stock.

Invoice. The bill for merchandise from a supplier that you use to pay for the merchandise you purchase from them. Not to be confused with statements, which are sent out monthly by some vendors, summarizing previous invoices and payments. Most vendors expect payment from the invoice.

Keystone. A retailing term for a 50 percent markup, which is equivalent to doubling the cost of goods to determine the selling price.

Layaway. Allowing customers to pay off a purchase over time, while you retain the goods. Normally requires payments over a relatively short period such as three months, with 25 percent down and three subsequent equal payments.

Lessee. You, as the renter of a space.

Lessor. The person or company from whom you rent.

Liability. Accounting term for debts your business owes, such as outstanding loans or accounts payable.

Market center. A regional wholesale center, where vendors and manufacturers display and sell their goods to you, the retailer. A sort of retail store for retailers, usually located in larger cities.

Markup. The percent of the selling price of an item that constitutes your gross profit. For example, an item that you sell for $1.00, for which you paid $0.75, would have a 25 percent markup. Remember that markup is figured on the selling price, not the cost.

Minimum. The smallest amount of goods a supplier will allow you to purchase, usually a dollar amount, but sometimes a quantity.

Net 30. Credit terms extended by a supplier, meaning you must pay the full amount within 30 days of shipment.

Net profit. Your gross profit, as defined above, less your expenses.

Payroll taxes. The taxes you must collect and pay based on a percentage of the gross wages of an employee. Always includes social security, Medicare, and federal unemployment tax, and usually includes state unemployment and other state, and sometimes local, taxes.

Profit and loss (P&L) statement. A financial report showing your sales, cost of goods, gross profits, and net profits for a given period.

Sales tax. A tax you must collect and remit to a state or local government, usually a percent of gross sales. Only a handful of states do not levy a state sales tax.

Security deposit. A payment, usually one or more month's rent, normally demanded by lessors to protect them for any damages you may cause to their premises. It is refundable upon vacating the leased space.

Shopping mall. An enclosed, climate-controlled shopping area containing many varied stores, and typically anchored by two or more major department stores.

Single-entry bookkeeping. A simplified accounting system in which each expense or income item is entered only once. Does not provide the checks and balances and uniformity of a double-entry system.

Strip shopping center. A small group of stores joined together in a building, usually fronting a major thoroughfare. They usually have a common parking area, but each store has access to the street or common area.

Triple-net. A variable charge frequently added to your rent by lessors to cover taxes, insurance, and common-area maintenance.

Unemployment tax. A payroll tax levied by state and federal governments to finance payments to unemployed workers.

Withholding taxes. Amounts you are required to withhold from employees' wages for social security, Medicare, and income taxes, and deposit with the IRS. You must also withhold state income taxes and deposit these with your state's department of revenue. The taxes you withhold are in addition to the payroll taxes you must pay as an employer.

Appendix B

Resources

Magazines

Staying well-informed about local, state, and national business and buying trends can often mean the difference between success and failure. As a retail business owner, you will want to be informed of the newest, most innovative products for your store as well as keep an eye out for what is hot on a national level.

Local newspapers and state-specific magazines are valuable sources of local business news, but to stay in touch with nationwide business trends, consider subscribing to several national business publications. The magazines below represent only a sampling of the myriad publications that cover general business issues and specialty retailing and merchandise lines.

Trade magazines for specialty areas of retailing abound and are constantly changing. The most effective way to locate magazines that fit your proposed area of retail is to search the internet. One site that handles an array of publications for retailing is: www .tradepublications.com.

If you cannot locate what you need there, try searching the internet using Yahoo or one of the other search engines and a key-word describing your retailing interest and the word "publication." A few sample magazines that cover more general retailing areas are listed below.

Smart Retailer
707 Kautz Road
St. Charles, IL 60174
(888) 228-7624
This magazine provides business management expertise for retailers specializing in gift merchandise. Not only is it a source for business advice, but also a wholesale buying resource. Articles cover successful marketing and merchandising techniques, industry trends, and new products.

Entrepreneur
2445 McCabe Way
Irvine, CA 92614
(949) 261-2325
This monthly publication features information on running a small business. Contains management tips, entrepreneurial success stories, franchise information, and news and reviews of the latest in office equipment.

Giftware News
233 N. Michigan Ave., Suite 1780
Chicago, IL 60610
voice: (312) 849-2220
This publication is written for gift, stationery, and department stores, as well as other retail outlets that sell giftware, stationery, tabletop and decorative accessories. New products, innovations in marketing and retailing techniques, and new trends in consumer buying comprise the regular features. Previews of major market shows are provided.

Inc. Magazine
7 World Trade Center
New York, NY 10007-2195
(212) 389-5377
This monthly publication emphasizes the critical contribution of the small firm to the American economy. *Inc.* provides managers of small to midsized privately held companies with information on management approaches in finance, marketing, and personnel, as well as profiles of leading growth companies and analyses of economic and policy trends affecting the contemporary small growth firm.

Books and Other Publications

Circular E, Employer's Tax Guide
Internal Revenue Service (IRS)
Washington, DC
(800) 829-3676
An IRS publication that explains federal income tax withholding and social security tax requirements for employers. *Circular E* also contains up-to-date withholding tax tables so you can determine how much federal income tax and social security tax to withhold from employee paychecks.

How Do I Customer Guides
U. S. Citizenship and Immigration Services (USCIS)
1 (800) 375-5283
TTY 1 (800) 767-1833
These are online guides for hiring employees and maintaining compliance with immigration and Homeland Security laws.

The Legal Guide for Starting and Running a Small Business
Nolo Press
950 Parker Street
Berkeley, CA 94710-2524

The new edition of *The Legal Guide for Starting and Running a Small Business* features a comprehensive, four-page checklist of everything you should do to start a new business.

Small-Time Operator
Bell Springs Publishing
Box 1240
Willits, CA 95490
(707) 459-6372
Overall general startup book written in everyday language that tackles the technical aspects of starting a business. It is also a workbook that includes bookkeeping instructions and a sample set of ledgers—all especially designed for the small business owner.

Small Business Administration Resources

The federal Small Business Administration (SBA) is one government agency that is genuinely helpful to small businesses. Among other services—such as providing free seminars and workshops, small business financing, and telephone hotlines—the SBA has online resources that you may find helpful. Among them are:

Management and Planning Series
1. Checklist for Going Into Business MP-12
2. Selecting the Legal Structure for Your Business MP-25
3. Evaluating Franchise Opportunities MP-26
4. Handbook for Small Business MP-31
5. How to Write a Business Plan MP-32

Financial Management Series
1. ABC's of Borrowing FM-1
2. A Venture Capital Primer for Small Business FM-5
3. Budgeting in a Small Service Firm FM-8
4. Financing for Small Business FM-14

Marketing Series
1. Marketing for Small Business: An Overview MT-2
2. Researching Your Market MT-8
3. Selling by Mail Order MT-9

Products/Ideas/Inventions Series
1. Ideas Into Dollars PI-1
2. Avoiding Patent, Trademark, and Copyright Problems PI-2
3. Trademarks and Business Goodwill PI-3

Contact the SBA at: www.sba.gov
SBA Answer Desk
1-800-U-ASK-SBA (1-800-827-5722)
Send emails to: answerdesk@sba.gov
Answer Desk TTY: (704) 344-6640
Free online training is available for many of the subject areas listed above.

Market, Gift, and Design Centers

The centers listed below are at fixed locations around the United States. In addition to gifts, most of the major centers also include, or are adjacent to, markets handling jewelry, apparel, furniture, home accessories, gourmet foods, kitchenware, and textiles.

Atlanta Market Center
240 Peachtree Street NW, Suite 2200
Atlanta, GA 30303
(800) ATL-MART

Chicago Merchandise Mart
222 Merchandise Mart Plaza
Chicago, IL 60654
(800) 677-6278

The Columbus Gift Mart
7001 Discovery Boulevard
Columbus, OH 43017
(888) 332-8979

Dallas Market Center
2100 Stemmons Freeway
Dallas, TX 75207
(214) 744-7444

Denver Merchandise Mart
451 East 58th Avenue
Denver, CO 80216
(303) 292-6278

New York Market Center
230 Fifth Avenue
New York, NY 10001
(800) 698-5617

International Home Furnishings Center
209 S. Main Street
High Point, NC 27260
(336) 888-3700

Gift Mart of Kansas City
9517 B Metcalf Avenue
Overland Park, KS 66212
(913) 687-8059

The L.A. Gift Mart
1933 S. Broadway
Los Angeles, CA 90007
(800) LAMART4

Miami International Merchandise Mart
777 NW 72nd Avenue
Miami, FL 33126
(305) 269-4811

Minneapolis Mart
10301 Bren Road West
Minnetonka, MN 55343
(952) 932-7200
(800) 626-1298

New York Merchandise Mart
41 Madison Avenue
New York, NY 10010
(212) 686-1203

Pittsburg Expo Mart
105 Mall Boulevard
Monroeville, PA 15146
(888) 968-3944

Tupelo Furniture Market
1879 Coley Road
Tupelo, MS 38801
(662) 842-4442

Appendix D

Exhibition Companies and Trade Associations

Trade associations represent specific segments of the retailing industry and can provide information about suppliers of specific goods. Exhibition management companies manage and stage periodic wholesale shows around the United States. These shows cover a broad spectrum of geography and merchandise and are usually held during the same period each year. They do not always have a permanent facility, but use local exhibition halls, auditoriums, and even hotel convention facilities.

The Market Square Traditional Wholesale Shows, for example, have winter and summer shows around Valley Forge, Pennsylvania, using several hotels and local exhibition halls around Philadelphia. Many of the companies sponsor several shows at different times and places.

Following is a sampling of trade associations and exhibition companies that deal in the retail industry. Since the names, locations, addresses, and telephone numbers for these groups change periodically, your best resource for zeroing in on your own special interest is the internet. Use a search engine and a keyword or words that describe your area of interest. If you want to locate a specific trade association or exhibition company, use Yahoo's

Yellow Pages or a similar source on one of the other search engines on the internet.

AMC Trade Shows, Ltd., A Portman Co.

American Association of Exporters and Importers, Inc.

American Craft Council

Art Buyers Caravan Trade Show

Association of Crafts & Creative Industries

Beckman's Gift Show Industry Productions of America, Inc.

Chicago Giftware Association

Douglas Trade Shows

The Fragrance Foundation

George Little Management

Greeting Card Association

International Mass Retailer Association

Jewelers of America, Inc.

Juvenile Products Manufacturers Association

Karel Expositions

Market Square Wholesale

National Association for the Specialty Food Trade, Inc.

National Association of Bridal Consultants

National Bridal Service

National Candle Association

National Housewares Association

National Luggage Dealers Association

National Retail Federation

National Tabletop & Giftware Association

OASIS Gift Show

Progressive Exhibitors, Inc.

The Rosen Group

Salt Lake Gift Show

Toy Manufacturers of America, Inc.

Urban Expositions

Western Exhibitors, Inc.

www.biztradeshows.com provides current listings for upcoming trade and wholesale shows

Index